Spiritual Leadership is the best book I've read on Christian leadership. I give copies to every key associate.

—Charles W. Colson
Chairman, Prison Fellowship

As a young pastor, J. Oswald Sanders' book *Spiritual Leadership* was the first book I read that awakened me to the subject of leadership. It started me on a 30-plus year journey of teaching leadership to pastors and laypeople. No other book has influenced my life the way this one has.

—John C. Maxwell
Author, speaker, and founder
the INJOY Group

Spiritual Leadership should be the constant companion of every under-shepherd in the Savior's service. Most helpful is the fact that its emphasis is not on methods, but on character, passion, and godliness. I read it often to regrip the basic perspectives of my task, and have given it to the entire leadership team in our church.

—John MacArthur
Pastor-teacher
Grace Community Church

I first read Oswald Sanders' *Spiritual Leadership* as a young woman heading into ministry. It helped to shape my perspective, priorities, and passion and to ground my heart and mind in the timeless truths of Scripture. Anyone who desires to serve the Lord would do well to digest and internalize this classic.

Many Christian workers today are enamored of the latest trends, marketing models, and bestselling books by leadership gurus; they aspire to a sense of greatness and success that exalts human giftedness and rests on shifting sand. By contrast, the kingdom of God will always and only be advanced by humble servants of God who lead out of a clear sense of divine calling, personal integrity, spiritual depth, and dependence on Christ—men and women of prayer, full of the Word and wisdom, and anointed with the power of the Spirit. These are the ingredients Sanders urges us to prize and pursue.

—Nancy Leigh DeMoss
Author, Host of *Revive Our Hearts* radio

SPIRITUAL LEADERSHIP

A Commitment to Excellence for Every Believer

J. OSWALD
SANDERS

MOODY PUBLISHERS
CHICAGO

Produced for Moody Publishers with the assistance of The Livingstone Corporation. Text updated by Mark Fackler, Ph.D. Study guide by James C. Galvin, Ed.D. and Neil Wilson. www.LivingstoneCorp.com

Cover Design: Brand Navigation, LLC—DeAnna Pierce, Terra Petersen, Bill Chiaravalle
(www.brandnavigation.com)
Interior Design: The Livingstone Corporation

ISBN: 0-8024-8227-9
ISBN-13: 978-0-8024-8227-3

We hope you enjoy this book from Moody Publishers. Our goal is to provide high-quality, thought-provoking books and products that connect truth to your real needs and challenges. For more information on other books and products written and produced from a biblical perspective, go to www.moodypublishers.com or write to:

Moody Publishers
820 N. LaSalle Boulevard
Chicago, IL 60610

9 10 8

Printed in the United States of America

CONTENTS

8.99 IN

PREFACE TO THE UPDATED EDITION

Over the span of forty years, Oswald Sanders's *Spiritual Leadership* has earned recognition as a classic study of the biblical principles of godly leadership. Originally a series of lectures delivered to leaders of the Overseas Missionary Fellowship, the book has been valued by thousands of readers for its keen insights and godly wisdom. So why the need for a line-by-line revision? Our concern was that the language of the original edition was making it increasingly difficult to appreciate the power of Sanders's ideas. Contemporary Christians who would otherwise benefit greatly from the book might be confused by references to obscure personalities, outdated expressions, and an absence of acknowledgment of more recent developments within the church and culture.

Our purpose, then, was to revise *Spiritual Leadership* for Christians living in the twenty-first century. We cannot improve on Sanders's insights, but we have attempted to update his writing by examining each sentence for its clarity and relevance to the contemporary reader. Although we have changed the wording extensively, we have remained faithful to the original meaning and intent of each passage. Some of the specific changes are described in the paragraphs below.

First, female leadership has always been a strong, if unsung, part of evangelical missions. In the original edition, almost no mention is made that women participate along with men in leading the world to Christ. Perhaps Sanders meant his references to "man," to "men," to "him," and to "his" to mean all people without respect to gender. It was common in his era to use masculine pronouns as a generic reference to everybody. But perhaps he did not. In any case, recognizing the role of both men and women in the church of Christ, we have enlarged the language of this second edition to include both, except in those specific parts where Sanders was obviously addressing only one group.

Second, we added notes to the text that identify many of the authorities whom Sanders cites, people now forgotten by most of us. Sanders quotes revivalists, preachers, scholars, and missionaries, often from the British church. He also admired and respected World War II military leaders whose names may or may not still be household words. Whenever possible, endnotes provide biographical information.

Finally, the text of the English Bible itself has undergone much change since Sanders spoke and wrote these pages. Except where otherwise noted, we have used *The New International Version* for the updated edition.

We trust the reader will "hear" these pages as well as read them. Like a good sermon, Sanders's points are often repeated; sometimes paragraphs contain forays beyond the main point; and final paragraphs of chapters often end quite abruptly, as if the speaker suddenly realized he was out of time and quickly wrapped up. Because this book was originally a series of lectures, we have tried to retain the feel and texture of the spoken word. We hope the reader will sense the immediacy and timelessness of these messages as much as the first audiences who heard them four decades ago.

PREFACE TO THE FIRST EDITION

This book had grown out of two series of messages delivered to the leaders of Overseas Missionary Fellowship at conferences in Singapore in 1964 and 1966. It was then suggested that these messages could be amplified and shared with a wider public. The author has acceded to this request.

The principles of leadership in both the temporal and spiritual realms are presented and illustrated in these pages from both Scripture and the lives of eminent men and women of God. Not every reader will have access to many of the biographies from which these illustrations are drawn, and this has encouraged the author to include pertinent incidents from the lives of persons whose leadership has been more than unusually successful. Whenever possible, sources are indicated. In the case of Scripture references, that translation has been used that appeared to the author to be most accurate and expressive.

The material has been presented in a form that is calculated to be of help even to younger Christians in whose hearts the Holy Spirit is working to create a holy ambition to place all their power at the disposal of the Redeemer. If there is something, too, that will rekindle aspirations and crystallize a fresh purpose in the hearts of those further along the road of leadership, the aim of the book will be realized.

J. Oswald Sanders

1
AN HONORABLE AMBITION

To aspire to leadership is an honorable ambition.
1 Timothy 3:1 NEB

Should you then seek great things for yourself? Seek them not.
Jeremiah 45:5

Most Christians have reservations about aspiring to leadership. They are unsure about whether it is truly right for a person to want to be a leader. After all, is it not better for the position to seek out the person rather than the person to seek out the position? Has not ambition caused the downfall of numerous otherwise great leaders in the church, people who fell victim to "the last infirmity of noble minds"? Shakespeare expressed a profound truth when his character Wolsey said to the great English general:

> *Cromwell, I charge thee, fling away ambitions,*
> *By that sin fell the angels; how can a man then,*
> *The image of his Maker, hope to profit by't?*

No doubt, Christians must resist a certain kind of ambition and rid it from their lives. But we must also acknowledge other ambitions as noble, worthy, and honorable. The two verses at the beginning of this chapter provide a warning—and an encouragement—for sorting out the difference. When our ambition carries out a burning desire to be effective in the service of God—to realize God's highest potential for our lives—we can keep both of these verses in mind and hold them in healthy tension.

Part of that tension is the difference between Paul's situation and ours. We may understand his statement (1 Timothy 3:1, above) in terms of the prestige and respect given to Christian leaders today. But such was far from Paul's mind. In his day, a bishop faced great danger and worrisome responsibility. Rewards for the work of leading the church were hardship, contempt, rejection, and even death. The leader was first to draw fire in persecution, first in line to suffer.

Seen in this light, Paul's encouragement does not seem so open to misuse by people merely seeking status in the church. Phonies would have little heart for such a difficult assignment. Under the dangerous circumstances that prevailed in the first century, even stout-hearted Christians needed encouragement and incentive to lead. And so Paul called leadership an "honorable ambition."

We ought never to forget that the same situation faces Christians today in certain parts of the world. Leaders of the church in China suffered most at the hands of Communists. The leader of the Little Flock in Nepal suffered years in prison after church members had been released. In many troubled areas today, spiritual leadership is no task for those who seek stable benefits and upscale working conditions. It remains true that any form of spiritual warfare will inevitably single out leaders who by their role present obvious targets.

Paul urges us to the work of leading within the church, the most important work in the world. When our motives are right, this work pays eternal dividends. In Paul's day, only a deep love for Christ and genuine concern for the church could motivate people to lead. But in many cultures today where Christian leadership carries prestige and privilege, people aspire to leadership for reasons quite unworthy and self-seeking. Holy ambition has always been surrounded by distortions.

And so we find the ancient prophet Jeremiah giving his servant Baruch some very wise and simple counsel: "Are you looking for great things for yourself? Don't do it." Jeremiah was not condemning all ambition as sinful, but he was pointing to selfish motivation that makes ambition wrong—"great things for yourself." Desiring to excel is not a sin. It is motivation that determines ambition's character. Our Lord never taught against the urge to high achievement, but He did expose and condemn unworthy motivation.

All Christians are called to develop God-given talents, to make the most of their lives, and to develop to the fullest their God-given gifts and capabilities. But Jesus taught that ambition that centers on the self is wrong. Speaking to young ministers about to be ordained, the great missionary leader Bishop Stephen Neill said: "I am inclined to think that ambition in any ordinary sense of the term is nearly always sinful in ordinary men. I am certain that in the Christian it is always sinful, and that it is most inexcusable of all in the ordained minister."[1]

Ambition which centers on the glory of God and welfare of the church is a mighty force for good.

The word *ambition* comes from a Latin word meaning "campaigning for promotion." The phrase suggests a variety of elements: social visibility and approval, popularity, peer recognition, the exercise of authority over others. Ambitious people, in this sense, enjoy the power that comes with money, prestige, and authority. Jesus had no time for such ego-driven ambitions. The true spiritual leader will never "campaign for promotion."

To His "ambitious" disciples Jesus announced a new standard of greatness: "You know that those who are regarded as rulers of the Gentiles lord it over them, and their high officials exercise authority over them. Not so with you. Instead, whoever wants to become great among you must be your servant, and whoever wants to be first must be slave of all" (Mark 10:42–44). We will consider this amazing statement at length in a later chapter. Here at the outset of this study of spiritual leadership, we will simply highlight Jesus' master principle: True greatness, true leadership, is found in giving yourself in service to others, not in coaxing or inducing others to serve you. True service is never without cost. Often it comes with a bitter cup of challenges and a painful baptism of suffering. For genuine godly leadership weighs carefully Jesus' question: "Can you drink the cup I drink or be baptized with the baptism I am baptized with?" (Mark 10:38b). The real spiritual leader is focused on the service he and she can render to God and other people, not on the residuals and perks of high office or holy title. We must aim to put more into life than we take out.

"One of the outstanding ironies of history is the utter disregard of ranks and titles in the final judgments men pass on each other," said Samuel Brengle, the great Salvation Army revival preacher. "The final estimate of men shows that history cares not an iota for the rank or title a man has borne, or the office he has held, but only the quality of his deeds and the character of his mind and heart."[2]

"Let it once be fixed that a man's ambition is to fit into God's plan for him, and he has a North Star ever in sight to guide him steadily over any sea, however shoreless it seems," wrote S. D. Gordon in one of his well-known devotional books. "He has a compass that points true in the thickest fog and fiercest storm, and regardless of magnetic rocks."

The great leader Count Nikolaus von Zinzendorf (1700–1760) was tempted by rank and riches; indeed, he is most widely known by the title of honor noted here. But his attitude toward ambition was summed up in one simple statement: "I have one passion: it is He, He alone." Zinzendorf turned from self-seeking to become the founder and leader of the Moravian church. His followers learned from their leader and circled the world with his passion. Before missionary work was popular or well-organized, the Moravians established overseas churches that had three times as many members as did their churches back home—a most unusual accomplishment. Indeed, one of every ninety-two Moravians left home to serve as a missionary.

> *Because we children of Adam want to become great,*
> *He became small.*
> *Because we will not stoop,*
> *He humbled Himself.*
> *Because we want to rule,*
> *He came to serve.*

FOR REFLECTION

A. How would you illustrate the differences between self-centered and God-centered ambition from your own life?

B. Who has been your most influencial example of godly leadership?

C. What are some areas of honorable/holy ambition in your life?

2
THE SEARCH
FOR LEADERS

No one from the east or the west
or from the desert can exalt a man.
But it is God who judges:
He brings one down, he exalts another.
Psalm 75:6–7

Give me a man of God—one man,
One mighty prophet of the Lord,
And I will give you peace on earth,
Bought with a prayer and not a sword.
George Liddell[1]

Real leaders are in short supply. Constantly people and groups search for them. A question echoes in every corner of the church—"Who will lead?" Throughout the Bible, God searches for leaders too.

"The LORD has sought out a man after his own heart and appointed him leader of his people" (1 Samuel 13:14).

"Go up and down the streets of Jerusalem, look around and consider, search through her squares. If you can find one person who deals honestly and seeks truth, I will forgive this city" (Jeremiah 5:1).

"I looked for a man among them who would build up the wall" (Ezekiel 22:30).

The Bible shows us that when God does find a person who is ready to lead, to commit to full discipleship, and take on responsibility for others, that person is used to the limit. Such leaders still have shortcomings and flaws, but despite those limitations, they serve God as spiritual leaders. Such were Moses, Gideon, and David. And in the history of the church, Martin Luther, John Wesley, Adoniram Judson, William Carey, and many others.

To be a leader in the church has always required strength and faith beyond the merely average. Why is our need for leaders so great, and candidates for leadership so few? Every generation faces the stringent demands of spiritual leadership, and most unfortunately turn away. But God welcomes the few who come forward to serve.

"The church is painfully in need of leaders," lamented the English Methodist preacher William Sangster. "I wait to hear a voice and no voice comes. I would rather listen than speak—but there is no clarion voice to listen to."[2]

If the world is to hear the church's voice today, leaders are needed who are authoritative, spiritual, and sacrificial. Authoritative, because people desire reliable leaders who know where they are going and are confident of getting there. Spiritual, because without a strong relationship to God, even the most attractive and competent person cannot lead people to God. Sacrificial, because this trait follows the model of Jesus, who gave Himself for the whole world and who calls us to follow in His steps.

Churches grow in every way when they are guided by strong, spiritual leaders with the touch of the supernatural radiating in their service. The church sinks into confusion and malaise without such leadership. Today those who preach with majesty and spiritual power are few, and the booming voice of the church has become a pathetic whisper. Leaders today—those who are truly spiritual—must take to heart their responsibility to pass on the torch to younger people as a first-line duty.

Many people regard leaders as naturally gifted with intellect, personal forcefulness, and enthusiasm. Such qualities certainly enhance leadership potential, but they do not define the spiritual leader. True leaders must be willing to suffer for the sake of objectives great enough to demand their wholehearted obedience.

Spiritual leaders are not elected, appointed, or created by synods or churchly assemblies. God alone makes them. One does not become a spiritual leader by merely filling an office, taking course work in the subject, or resolving in one's own will to do this task. A person must qualify to be a spiritual leader.

Often truly authoritative leadership falls on someone who years earlier dedicated themselves to practice the discipline of seeking first the kingdom of God. Then, as that person matures, God confers a leadership role, and the Spirit of God goes to work through him. When God's searching eye finds a person qualified to lead, God anoints that person with the Holy Spirit and calls him or her to a special ministry (Acts 9:17; 22:21).

Samuel Brengle, a gifted leader who served for many years in the Salvation Army, outlined the road to spiritual authority and leadership:

> It is not won by promotion, but my many prayers and tears. It is attained by confession of sin, and much heart-searching and humbling before God; by self-surrender, a courageous sacrifice of every idol, a bold uncomplaining embrace of the cross, and by eternally looking unto Jesus crucified. It is not gained by seeking great things for ourselves, but like Paul, by counting those things that are gain to us as loss for Christ. This is a great price, but it must be paid by the leader whose power is recognized and felt in heaven, on earth, and in hell.[3]

God wants to show such people how strong He really is (2 Chronicles 16:9). But not all who aspire to leadership are willing to pay such a high personal price. Yet there is no compromise here: in the secret reaches of the heart, this price is paid, before any public office or honor. Our Lord made clear to James and John that high position in the kingdom of God is reserved for those whose hearts—even the secret places where no one else probes—are qualified. God's sovereign searching of our hearts, and then His call to leadership, are awesome to behold. And they make a person very humble.

One last thing must be said, a kind of warning. If those who hold influence over others fail to lead toward the spiritual uplands, then surely the path to the lowlands will be well worn. People travel together;

no one lives detached and alone. We dare not take lightly God's call to leadership in our lives.

FOR REFLECTION

A. God took eighty years to prepare Moses for his leadership task. In what ways has God been preparing you?

B. As you begin this study, what do you understand as the primary qualifying traits of godly leadership?

C. How are you affected by the closing warning in this chapter?

3

THE MASTER'S
MASTER PRINCIPLE

Whoever wants to become great among you must be your servant,
and whoever wants to be first must be slave of all.

Mark 10:43–44

Given the importance of competent leaders in the church—and in business and government too—we might expect that the Bible would use the term more often. In fact, the King James Bible (on which many of my generation have been nurtured) uses *leader* only six times. Much more frequently, the role is called *servant*. We do not read about "Moses, my leader," but "Moses, my servant." And this is exactly what Christ taught.[1]

Jesus was a revolutionary, not in the guerrilla warfare sense but in His teaching on leadership. He overturned an existing order. In the world's ears, the term *servant* spoke everywhere of low prestige, low respect, low honor. Most people were not attracted to such a low-value role. When Jesus used the term, however, it was a synonym for greatness. And that was a revolutionary idea. It still is!

Christ taught that the kingdom of God was a community where each member served the others. He defined His ultimate purpose using that term:

"For even the Son of Man did not come to be served, but to serve, and to give his life as a ransom for many" (Mark 10:45). Paul wrote in the same vein: "Serve one another in love" (Galatians 5:13). Our loving service should spread also to the needy world around us. But in most churches, a few people carry the load.

Jesus knew that the idea of leader as "loving servant of all" would not appeal to most people. Securing our own creature comforts is a much more common mission. But "servant" is His requirement for those who want to lead in His kingdom.

The sharp contrast between our common ideas about leadership and the revolution Jesus announced is nowhere clearer than in the Gospel of Mark 10:42–43: "You know that those who are regarded as rulers of the Gentiles lord it over them, and their high officials exercise authority over them. Not so with you. Instead, whoever wants to become great among you must be your servant, and whoever wants to be the first must be slave of all."

This was such a revolutionary idea that even those closest to Jesus, the disciples James and John, used their ambitious mother in a scheme to secure top positions in the coming kingdom before the other ten received their due. These two disciples took very seriously Jesus' promise about sitting on glorious thrones and judging the tribes of Israel (Matthew 19:28), but they misunderstood how to get there.

Despite their friendship, Jesus did not give an inch to their campaign for office. "You don't know what you are asking," was His reply (Matthew 20:22). James and John wanted the glory, but not the cup of shame; the crown, but not the cross; the role of master, but not servant. Jesus used this occasion to teach two principles of leadership that the church must never forget.

- *The sovereignty principle of spiritual leadership.* "To sit at my right or left is not for me to grant. These places belong to those for whom they have been prepared" (Mark 10:40).

A more common response might have been: Honor and rank is for those who have prepared themselves for it, and worked very hard to get it. But here we see the fundamental difference in Jesus' teaching and our human ideas. God assigns places of spiritual ministry and leadership in His sovereign will. The New Living Translation makes the point of verse 40 very clear: "God has prepared those places for the one he has chosen."

Effective spiritual leadership does not come as a result of theological training or seminary degree, as important as education is. Jesus told His disciples, "You did not choose me, but I chose you and appointed you" (John 15:16). The sovereign selection of God gives great confidence to Christian workers. We can truly say, "I am here neither by selection of an individual nor election of a group but by the almighty appointment of God."

- *The suffering principle of spiritual leadership.* "Can you drink the cup I drink and be baptized with the baptism I am baptized with?" (Mark 10:38).

No hedging here. No dodging the hard realities. Jesus simply and honestly set forth the cost of serving in His kingdom. The task was magnificent and difficult; men and women leading in that task must have eyes wide open, and hearts willing to follow the Master all the way.

To the Lord's probing question, the disciples responded glibly, "We are able." What tragic lack of perspective! But Jesus knew what lay ahead. They would indeed drink the cup and know the baptism. They would fail miserably and be restored gloriously. Eventually, James would be executed, and John would finish his days in isolated confinement.

If the disciples figured to learn about leadership on the fast track and with appropriate perks and bonuses, Jesus soon disillusioned them. What a shock it was to discover that greatness comes through servanthood, and leadership through becoming a slave of all.

Only once in all the recorded words of Jesus did our Lord announce that He had provided an "example" for the disciples, and that was when He washed their feet (John 13:15). Only once in the rest of the New Testament does a writer offer an "example" (1 Peter 2:21), and that is an example of suffering. Serving and suffering are paired in the teaching and life of our Lord. One does not come without the other. And what servant is greater than the Lord?

The Spirit of Servanthood

Jesus' teaching on servanthood and suffering was not intended merely to inspire good behavior. Jesus wanted to impart the spirit of servanthood, the sense of personal commitment and identity that He expressed when He said, "I am among you as one who serves." Mere acts of service could be performed with motives far from spiritual.

In Isaiah 42, we read about the attitudes and inner motives that the coming Messiah would demonstrate as the ideal servant of the Lord. Where Israel failed to live up to this ideal, the Messiah would succeed. And the principles of His life would be a pattern for ours.

Dependence. "Here is my servant, whom I uphold" (Isaiah 42:1). This verse speaks of the coming Messiah. Jesus fulfilled the prophecy by emptying Himself of divine prerogative ("made himself nothing," Philippians 2:7). He surrendered the privileges of His God-nature and became dependent on His heavenly Father. He became in all ways like a human being. What a staggering paradox. As we become "empty" of self and dependent on God, the Holy Spirit will use us.

Approval. "My chosen one in whom I delight"(Isaiah 42:1). God took great delight in His servant Jesus. On at least two occasions, God declared that delight audibly (Matthew 3:17; 17:5). And that delight was reciprocal. In another Old Testament reference to the coming Messiah, the Son testifies,"I delight to do thy will, O my God" (Psalm 40:8 KJV).

Modesty. "He will not shout or cry out, or raise his voice in the streets" (Isaiah 42:2). Neither strident nor flamboyant, God's servant conducts a ministry that appears almost self-effacing. What a contrast to the arrogant self-advertising of so many hypesters today, both in and out of the church.

On this very point the devil tempted Jesus, urging Him to attempt a headline-grabbing leap from the rooftop of the temple (Matthew 4:5). But Jesus did not seek headlines and did not fall to the plot.

So quiet and unobtrusive is the great Servant's work that many today doubt His very existence. Jesus exemplifies the description of God found later in Isaiah: "Truly you are a God who hides himself" (Isaiah 45:15). This quality seems to be shared among all the host of heaven. Even the picture given to us of the cherubim—God's angel servants—use four of their six wings to conceal their faces and feet. They too are content with hidden service (Isaiah 6:2).

Empathy. "A bruised reed he will not break, and a smoldering wick he will not snuff out" (Isaiah 42:3). The Lord's servant is sympathetic with the weak, mercifully understanding toward those who err. How often do people who fail wear the treadmarks of fellow pilgrims? But the ideal Servant does not trample on the weak and failing. He mends bruises and fans the weak spirit into a flame. Those who follow in His steps will never walk over people.

Many of us, even Christian workers, see a person whose life is a wreck and "pass by on the other side." We seek a ministry more rewarding and worthy of our talents than bearing up the frail side of humanity. But from God's point of view, it is noble work to reclaim the world's downtrodden people. When we find some of those the world calls "the least" and seek to meet their needs, Christ tells us we can think of them as Him (Matthew 25:45).

How dimly Peter's own wick burned in the garden and the judgment hall, but what a blaze on the day of Pentecost! God's ideal Servant made that miserable man's life a brilliant flame.

Optimism. "He will not falter or be discouraged till he establishes justice on earth" (Isaiah 42:4). Pessimism and leadership are at opposite ends of life's attitudes. Hope and optimism are essential qualities for the servant of God who battles with the powers of darkness over the souls of men and women. God's ideal Servant is optimistic until every part of God's work is done.

Anointing. "I will put my spirit on him" (Isaiah 42:1). None of these leadership qualities—dependence, approval, modesty, empathy, or optimism—are sufficient for the task. Without the touch of the supernatural, these qualities are dry as dust. And so the Holy Spirit comes to rest upon and dwell in the ideal Servant. "You know . . . how

God anointed Jesus of Nazareth with the Holy Spirit and power, and how he went around doing good" (Acts 10:38). Jesus' ministry began when the Spirit descended at His baptism, and then how the Servant began to shake the world!

Are we greater than our Lord? Can we do effective ministry without the Spirit of God working through us at every step? God offers us the same anointing. May we follow close to the great Servant, and receive the Spirit who shows us more of the Master.

FOR REFLECTION

A. How can you tell when you are being a servant?

B. What examples would you use to explain the sovereignty and suffering principles of spiritual leadership to someone?

C. Isaiah 42 includes six characteristics of God's special servant, Jesus. Which one do you find the greatest challenge as you exercise leadership?

4
NATURAL AND
SPIRITUAL
LEADERSHIP

*When I came to you . . . my message and my preaching were not with wise
and persuasive words, but with a demonstration of the Spirit's power.*

1 Corinthians 2:1,4

Leadership is influence, the ability of one person to influence others to follow his or her lead. Famous leaders have always known this.

The great military leader Bernard Montgomery spoke of leadership in these terms: "Leadership is the capacity and will to rally men and women to a common purpose, and the character which inspires confidence."[1] An outstanding example of this statement was Sir Winston Churchill, leader of Britain during World War II.

Fleet Admiral Nimitz said: "Leadership may be defined as that quality that inspires sufficient confidence in subordinates as to be willing to accept his views and carry out his commands."

General Charles Gordon once asked Li Hung Chang, a leader in China, two questions: "What is leadership? And how is humanity divided?" Li Hung replied: "There are only three kinds of people—those who are immovable, those who are movable, and those who move them!" Leaders move others.

John R. Mott, a world leader in student ministries, believed that "a leader is a man who knows the road, who can keep ahead, and who pulls others after him."[2]

P. T. Chandapilla, an Indian student leader, defined Christian leadership as a vocation that blends both human and divine qualities in a harmony of ministry by God and His people for the blessing of others.[3]

President Harry S. Truman (1945–1953) said cogently: "A leader is a person who has the ability to get others to do what they don't want to do, and like it."

Spiritual leadership blends natural and spiritual qualities. Yet even the natural qualities are supernatural gifts, since all good things come from God. Take personality, for instance. Montgomery said that, "the degree of influence will depend on the personality, the 'incandescence' of which the leader is capable, the flame which burns within, the magnetism which will draw the hearts of others toward him."[4] Both natural and spiritual qualities reach their greatest effectiveness when employed in the service of God and for His glory.

Yet spiritual leadership transcends the power of personality and all other natural gifts. The personality of the spiritual leader influences others because it is penetrated, saturated, and empowered by the Holy Spirit. As the leader gives control of his life to the Spirit, the Spirit's power flows through him to others.

Spiritual leadership requires superior spiritual power, which can never be generated by the self. There is no such thing as a self-made spiritual leader. A true leader influences others spiritually only because the Spirit works in and through him to a greater degree than in those he leads.

We can lead others only as far along the road as we ourselves have traveled. Merely pointing the way is not enough. If we are not walking, then no one can be following, and we are not leading anyone.

At a large meeting of mission leaders in China, the discussion turned to leadership and its qualifications. The debate was vigorous. But through it all, one person sat quietly listening. Then the chair asked if D. E. Hoste, general director of China Inland Mission, had an opinion. The auditorium became still.

With a twinkle in his eye, Hoste said in his high-pitched voice: "It occurs to me that perhaps the best test of whether one is qualified to lead, is to find out whether anyone is following."[5]

Born or Made?

Are leaders born or made? Surely, both. On the one hand, leadership is an "elusive and electric quality" that comes directly from God. On the other, leadership skills are distributed widely among every community, and should be cultivated and developed. Often our skills lie dormant until a crisis arises.

Some people become leaders by opportunity and timing. A crisis comes, no one better qualified steps forward, and a leader is born. But closer investigation usually reveals that the selection was less fortuitous and more the result of hidden training that made the person fit for leadership. Joseph is a perfect example (Genesis 37–45). He became prime minister of Egypt through circumstances that most people would call "lucky stars." In fact his promotion was the outcome of thirteen years of rigorous, hidden training under the hand of God.

When we contrast natural and spiritual leadership, we see just how different they are.

Natural	Spiritual
Self-confident	Confident in God
Knows men	Also knows God
Makes own decisions	Seeks God's will
Ambitious	Humble
Creates methods	Follows God's example
Enjoys command	Delights in obedience to God
Seeks personal reward	Loves God and others
Independent	Depends on God

People without natural leadership skills do not become great leaders at the moment of conversion. Yet a review of the history of the church reveals that the Holy Spirit sometimes releases gifts and qualities that were dormant beforehand. When that happens, a leader is born. A. W. Tozer wrote:

> *A true and safe leader is likely to be one who has no desire to lead, but is forced into a position by the inward leading of the Holy Spirit and the press of circumstances. . . . There was hardly a great leader from Paul to the present day but was drafted by the Holy Spirit for the task, and commissioned by the Lord to fill a position he had little heart for. . . . The man who is ambitious to lead is disqualified. . . . the true leader will have no desire to lord it over God's heritage, but will be humble, gentle, self-sacrificing and altogether ready to follow when the Spirit chooses another to lead.*[6]

Sangster's biography includes a private manuscript written when the English preacher and scholar felt a growing conviction to take more of a leadership role in the Methodist church.

> *This is the will of God for me. I did not choose it. I sought to escape it. But it has come. Something else has come, too. A sense of certainty that God does not want me only for a preacher. He wants me also for a leader. I feel a commissioning to work under God for the revival of this branch of His Church (Methodist)— careless of my own reputation; indifferent to the comments of older and jealous men. I am thirty-six. If I am to serve God in this way, I must no longer shrink from the task—but do it. I have examined my heart for ambition. I am certain it is not there. I hate the criticism I shall evoke and the painful chatter of people. Obscurity, quiet browsing among books, and the service of simple people is my taste—but by the will of God, this is my task, God help me.*
>
> *Bewildered and unbelieving, I hear the voice of God say to me: "I want to sound the note through you." O God, did ever an apostle shrink from his task more? I dare not say "no" but, like Jonah, I would fain run away.*[7]

Once Saint Francis of Assisi was confronted by a brother who asked him repeatedly, "Why you? Why you?"

Francis responded, in today's terms, "Why me *what?*"

"Why does everyone want to see you? Hear you? Obey you? You are not all so handsome, nor learned, nor from a noble family. Yet the world seems to want to follow you," the brother said.

Then Francis raised his eyes to heaven, knelt in praise to God, and turned to his interrogator:

> *You want to know? It is because the eyes of the Most High have*
> *willed it so. He continually watches the good and the wicked,*
> *and as His most holy eyes have not found among sinners any*
> *smaller man, nor any more insufficient and sinful, therefore He*
> *has chosen me to accomplish the marvelous work which God*
> *hath undertaken; He chose me because He could find none more*
> *worthless, and He wished to confound the nobility and grandeur,*
> *the strength, the beauty and the learning of this world.*[8]

Montgomery outlined seven qualities necessary for a military leader, each appropriate to spiritual warfare: the leader must 1) avoid getting swamped in detail; 2) not be petty; 3) not be pompous; 4) know how to select people to fit the task; 5) trust others to do a job without the leader's meddling; 6) be capable of clear decisions; 7) inspire confidence.[9]

John Mott spent time with students, and his tests emphasized youthful leadership development. One should inquire of a potential leader whether he or she 1) does little things well; 2) has learned to focus on priorities; 3) uses leisure well; 4) has intensity; 5) knows how to exploit momentum; 6) is growing; 7) overcomes discouragement and "impossible" situations; and 8) understands his or her weaknesses.[10]

A single life has immense possibilities for good or ill. We leave an indelible impact on people who come within our influence, even when we are not aware of it. Dr. John Geddie went to Aneityum (a Polynesian island) in 1848 and worked there for twenty-four years. Written in his memory are these words:

> *When he landed, in 1848, there were no Christians.*
> *When he left, in 1872, there were no heathen.*[11]

When the burning zeal of the early church began to draw converts at an extraordinary rate, the Holy Spirit taught a wonderful lesson on leadership. The church had too few leaders to care for all the needs, especially among the poor and the widows. Another echelon of leaders was needed. "Brothers, choose seven men from among you who are known to be full of the Spirit and wisdom. We will turn this responsibility over to them" (Acts 6:3).

These new leaders were first and foremost to be full of the Spirit. Spirituality is not easy to define, but you can tell when it is present. It is the fragrance of the garden of the Lord, the power to change the atmosphere around you, the influence that makes Christ real to others.

If deacons are required to be full of the Spirit, should those who preach and teach the Word of God be any less? Spiritual goals can be achieved only by spiritual people who use spiritual methods. How our churches and mission agencies would change if leaders were Spirit-filled! The secular mind and heart, however gifted and personally charming, has no place in the leadership of the church.

John Mott captured well the heart of spiritual leadership:

> *Leadership in the sense of rendering maximum service;*
> *leadership in the sense of the largest unselfishness; in the sense*
> *of full-hearted absorption in the greatest work of the world:*
> *building up the kingdom of our Lord Jesus Christ.*[12]

FOR REFLECTION

A. What qualities do you most look for in a leader? In what ways are you that kind of person?

B. What "natural" leadership abilities do you sense God has given or built into you?

C. Where do you fit in the chart of the Natural and Spiritual qualities on page 29?

5
CAN YOU BECOME
A LEADER?

Send some men to explore the land of Canaan. . . .
From each ancestral tribe send one of its leaders.

Numbers 13:2

Whe Jesus selected leaders, He ignored every popular idea of His day (and ours) about what kind of person could fit the role. Jesus' band of disciples started out untrained and without influence—a motley group for world change.

Any campaign for change today would have a star-studded cast of directors and advisers. In Jesus' group, where was the prominent statesman, the financier, the athlete, professor, or acclaimed clergy? Instead, Jesus looked for a humbler sort of person, unspoiled by the sophistication of His day.

Jesus chose from the ranks of workers, not professional clergy. When Hudson Taylor did the same thing, selecting mostly lay men and women for his missionary team to China, the religious world was shocked. Today that is a widely recognized, though not always approved, procedure.

Jesus chose people with little education, but they soon displayed remarkable flair. He saw in them something no one else did, and under His skillful hand they emerged as leaders who would shock the world. To their latent talents were added fervent devotion and fierce loyalty, honed in the school of failure and fatigue.

Natural leadership qualities are important. Too often these skills lie dormant and undiscovered. If we look carefully, we should be able to detect leadership potential. And if we have it, we should train it and use it for Christ's work. Here are some ways to investigate your potential:

- How do you identify and deal with bad habits? To lead others, you must master your appetites.

- How well do you maintain self-control when things go wrong? The leader who loses control under adversity forfeits respect and influence. A leader must be calm in crisis and resilient in disappointment.

- To what degree do you think independently? A leader must use the best ideas of others to make decisions. A leader cannot wait for others to make up his or her mind.

- How well can you handle criticism? When have you profited from it? The humble person can learn from petty criticism, even malicious criticism.

- Can you turn disappointment into creative new opportunity? What three actions could you take facing any disappointment?

- Do you readily gain the cooperation of others and win their respect and confidence? Genuine leadership doesn't have to manipulate or pressure others.

- Can you exert discipline without making a power play? Are your corrections or rebukes clear without being destructive? True leadership is an internal quality of the spirit and needs no show of external force.

- In what situations have you been a peacemaker? A leader must be able to reconcile with opponents and make peace where arguments have created hostility.

- Do people trust you with difficult and delicate matters? Your answer should include examples.

- Can you induce people to do happily some legitimate thing that they would not normally wish to do? Leaders know how to make others feel valued.

- Can you accept opposition to your viewpoint or decision without taking offense? Leaders always face opposition.

- Can you make and keep friends? Your circle of loyal friends is an index of your leadership potential.

- Do you depend on the praise of others to keep you going? Can you hold steady in the face of disapproval and even temporary loss of confidence?

- Are you at ease in the presence of strangers? Do you get nervous in the office of your superior? A leader knows how to exercise and accept authority.

- Are people who report to you generally at ease? A leader should be sympathetic and friendly.

- Are you interested in people? All types? All races? No prejudice?

- Are you tactful? Can you anticipate how your words will affect a person? Genuine leaders think before speaking.

- Is your will strong and steady? Leaders cannot vacillate, cannot drift with the wind. Leaders know there's a difference between conviction and stubbornness.

- Can you forgive? Or do you nurse resentments and harbor ill-feelings toward those who have injured you?

- Are you reasonably optimistic? Pessimism and leadership do not mix. Leaders are positively visionary.

- Have you identified a master passion such as that of Paul, who said, "This *one thing* I do!" Such singleness of motive will focus your energies and powers on the desired objective. Leaders need a strong focus.

- How do you respond to new responsibility?

How we handle relationships tells a lot about our potential for leadership. R. E. Thompson suggests these tests:

- Do other people's failures annoy or challenge you?

- Do you "use" people, or cultivate people?

- Do you direct people, or develop people?

- Do you criticize or encourage?

- Do you shun or seek the person with a special need or problem?[1]

These self-examinations mean little unless we act to correct our deficits and fill in the gaps of our training. Perhaps the final test of leadership potential is whether you "sit" on the results of such an analysis or do something about it. Why not take some of the points of weakness and failure you just identified or are already aware of and, in cooperation with the Holy Spirit, who is the Spirit of discipline, go into intentional character training. Concentrate on strengthening those areas of weakness and correcting faults.

Desirable qualities were present in all their fullness in the character of our Lord. Each Christian should make it his constant prayer that Christlikeness might more rapidly be incorporated into his or her own personality.

Adding leadership potential to our lives usually requires that we shake off negative elements that hold us back. If we are overly sensitive when criticized and rush to defend ourselves, that must go. If we make excuses for failure and try to blame others or circumstances, that must go. If we are intolerant or inflexible, so that creative people around us feel hemmed in, that must go.

If we are disturbed by anything short of perfection in ourselves and others, that must go. The perfectionist sets goals beyond his reach, then sinks into false guilt when he falls short. Our world is imperfect, and we cannot expect the impossible. Setting modest, realistic goals will help a perfectionist move through a problem without discouragement.

If you cannot keep a secret, do not try to lead. If you cannot yield a point when someone else's ideas are better, save yourself the frustration of failed leadership. If you want to maintain an image of infallibility, find something else to do besides leading people.

FOR REFLECTION

A. Pages 34–36 include twenty-two leadership potential measurements. Read through them again and as you think about them, put a (+) or (-) beside each one as it applies to your present exercise of leadership.

B. How would you answer the title of this chapter?

C. What was the most convicting, challenging, or surprising thought in this chapter?

6

INSIGHTS ON
LEADERSHIP
FROM PAUL

Now the overseer must be above reproach, the husband of but one wife,
temperate, self-controlled, respectable, hospitable, able to teach, not given to
drunkenness, not violent but gentle, not quarrelsome, not a lover of money.
He must manage his own family well and see that his children obey him with
proper respect. . . . He must not be a recent convert, or he may become
conceited. . . . He must also have a good reputation with outsiders.

1 Timothy 3:2–7

An architect friend once said to me as we looked at a building he had just completed, "It's humbling to see your own ideas suddenly standing as brick, mortar, and paint!" The comment reminded me of how much clearer are spiritual principles when we see them lived out in people instead of merely stating them in the abstract. Paul embodied principles of leadership that he also described in his letters. He certainly thought the life of individual believers and churches ought to resemble a solid foundation on Christ (see 1 Corinthians 3:9–17). Looking at Paul's life, we can see leadership all the more clearly.

The reputation of a great leader grows with the years. Surely Paul's moral and spiritual greatness is all the more evident the more he is studied and analyzed. A. W. Tozer called him the world's most successful Christian. It is sheer irony and miracle that God would select one of the most aggressive opponents of the early Christian movement and make him into its most outstanding leader.

Paul was uniquely equipped for the major role to which God called him. A present-day parallel to this amazing man would be someone who could speak in Chinese in Beijing, quoting Confucius and Mencius; write cogent theology and teach it at Oxford; and defend his cause using flawless Russian before the Soviet Academy of Sciences. By whatever comparison, Paul was certainly one of the most versatile leaders the church has known.

His versatility is apparent in the ease with which he adapted to various audiences. Paul could address statesmen and soldiers, adults and children, kings and royal officials. He was at ease in debate with philosophers, theologians, and pagan idol worshippers.

Paul had a brilliant grasp of the Old Testament. He studied under the influential rabbi Gamaliel, and as a student Paul was second to none. His own testimony records: "I was advancing in Judaism beyond many Jews of my own age and was extremely zealous for the traditions of my fathers" (Galatians 1:14).

A natural leader by any measure, Paul became a great spiritual leader when his heart and mind were captured by Jesus Christ.

Paul had boundless, Christ-centered ambition. His supreme love for Christ coupled with the obligation to share Christ's message were his powerful lifetime motives (Romans 1:14; 2 Corinthians 5:14). His authentic missionary passion helped him leap over all cultural and racial barriers. All people were his concern. A person's wealth or poverty, status or intellect had no bearing on Paul's concern for him.

In addition to his own schooling and experiences, Paul enjoyed the illumination and inspiration of the Holy Spirit. Qualities of leadership Paul taught are as relevant now as during the first century A.D. We dare not toss them off as antiquated or carelessly regard them as mere options.

The selection from 1 Timothy quoted at the head of this chapter spells out qualifications for spiritual leadership. Let us look at it again, and consider its parts.

Social Qualifications

With respect to relationships within the church, the leader is to be above reproach. Detractors should not have a rung to stand on. If a charge is preferred against him, it fails because his life affords no grounds for reproach or indictment of wrongdoing. His adversary finds no opening for a smear campaign, rumor mongering, or gossip.

With respect to relationships outside the church, the spiritual leader is to enjoy a good reputation. An elder known to the author was a businessman who often took preaching appointments on the Lord's Day. His employees used to say that they could tell when he had been preaching on Sunday because of his ill temper on Monday. Those outside the church can see plainly when our lives fall short of our testimony. We cannot hope to lead people to Christ by living an example of such contradiction.

Outsiders will criticize; nonetheless they respect the high ideals of Christian character. When a Christian leader full of high ideals lives a holy and joyful life in front of unbelievers, they often want to cultivate a similar experience. The character of the elder should command the respect of the unbeliever, inspire his confidence, and arouse his aspiration. Example is much more potent than precept.

Moral Qualifications

Moral principles common to the Christian life are under constant, subtle attack, and none more so than sexual faithfulness. The Christian leader must be blameless on this vital and often unpopular point. Faithfulness to one marriage partner is the biblical norm. The spiritual leader should be a man of unchallengeable morality.

The spiritual leader must be temperate, not addicted to alcohol. To be drunk is to show a disorderly personal life. Drunkenness is a disgrace anywhere, and much more so when it captures a Christian. A leader cannot allow a secret indulgence that would undermine public witness.

Mental Qualifications

A leader must be prudent, a person with sound judgment. This principle describes "the well-balanced state of mind resulting from habitual self-restraint"—the inner character that comes from daily self-discipline. Jeremy Taylor called this quality "reason's girdle and passion's bridle."[1] The ancient Greeks, who valued this quality, described it as a disciplined mind not swayed by sudden impulse or flying to extremes. For example, courage to the Greeks was the "golden mean" between rashness and timidity; purity was the mean between prudery and immorality. In a similar way, the Christian leader who possesses a sound mind has control of every part of his personality, habits, and passions.

As to behavior, the leader must be respectable. A well-ordered life is the fruit of a well-ordered mind. The life of the leader should reflect the beauty and orderliness of God.

Then the leader must be ready and able to teach. In a leader, watch for this desire, this spark. It creates opportunities to help others understand the meaning of spiritual life. The leader feels the joy of the Spirit and wants others to know God as well. Moreover, the leader's responsibility for teaching those under him should be supported by a blameless life.

Teaching is hard work, and doing it well takes time, preparation, study, and prayer. Samuel Brengle lamented:

> *Oh, for teachers among us; leaders who know how to read hearts and apply truth to the needs of the people, as a good physician reads patients and applies remedies to their ills. There are soul-sicknesses open and obscure, acute and chronic, superficial and deep-seated that the truth in Jesus will heal.*[2]

John Wesley had these gifts. He never indulged in a cheap disparagement of the intellect and was always trying to promote knowledge of the Scriptures and spiritual renewal among the people. He was intellectually gifted and possessed an impressive command of English literature. An eminent preacher declared that he knew of no sermons that gave greater evidence of an intimate knowledge of classical and general literature than those of Wesley. Yet he was widely known as a person "of one Book." That kind of breadth, focused on the Scriptures, is a high example of the consecrated intellect of the spiritual leader.

Personality Qualifications

If you would rather pick a fight than solve a problem, do not consider leading the church. The Christian leader must be genial and gentle, not a lover of controversy. R. C. Trench says that the leader should be one who corrects and "redresses the injustices of justice." Aristotle taught that the leader should be one who "remembers good rather than evil, the good one has received rather than the good one has done." The leader must be actively considerate, not merely passive and certainly not withdrawn but irenic in disposition, always seeking a peaceful solution, and able to diffuse an explosive situation.

Then the leader must show hospitality. This ministry should never be seen as an irksome imposition but rather as one that offers the privilege of service. *The Shepherd of Hermas*, a widely used book written in the second century A.D., mentions that a bishop "must be hospitable, a man who gladly and at all times welcomes into his house the servants of God."

When Paul wrote his letter to Timothy, inns were few, dirty, and known for their immoral atmosphere. Visiting Christians depended on open doors of hospitality. A friend of the author, a person with a rather large portfolio of business and church responsibilities, kept an "open home" policy for visitors and the underprivileged on each Lord's Day. It was a practice that enriched his life and blessed others, and demonstrated this important quality of spiritual leadership.

Covetousness and its twin, the love of money, disqualify a person for leadership. Financial reward cannot enter a leader's mind in the exercise of ministry. The leader must be as willing to accept an appointment with a lower remuneration as one with a higher.

Before going to Madeley, John Fletcher was told by his benefactor, Mr. Hill, that he could have a position in Dunham in Cheshire, where "the parish is small, the duty light, and the income good." Moreover it was "in fine sporting country!"

"Alas, sir," replied Fletcher, "Dunham will not suit me. There is too much money and too little labor."

"A pity to decline such a living," said Hill. "Would you like Madeley?"

"That, sir, would be the very place for me." And in that church the man who cared nothing for money had a remarkable ministry, still being felt in this generation.[3]

Domestic Qualifications

The Christian leader who is married must demonstrate the ability to "manage his own family well and see that his children obey him with proper respect" (1 Timothy 3:4). We cannot accept the picture of a stern, unsmiling patriarch, immune to laughter and impervious to emotion. But Paul urges a well-ordered home where mutual respect and supportive harmony are the keynotes. Failure to keep home in order has kept many ministers and missionaries from their fullest potential.

To reach this goal, a spouse must fully share the leader's spiritual aspirations and be willing to join in the necessary sacrifices. Many a gifted leader has been lost to high office and spiritual effectiveness because of an uncooperative spouse. Without a benevolent and happy discipline in one's home, can a Christian worker be expected to manage a ministry? Can hospitality be offered if children carry on without restraint? Can a ministry to other families be effective if one's own family is in disarray?

While a leader cares for church and mission, he must not neglect the family, which is his primary and personal responsibility. The discharge of one duty in God's kingdom does not excuse us from another. There is time for every legitimate duty. Paul implies that a person's ability to lead at home is a strong indicator of his readiness to lead in ministry.

Maturity

Spiritual maturity is indispensable to good leadership. A novice or new convert should not be pushed into leadership. A plant needs time to take root and come to maturity, and the process cannot be hurried. The seedling must take root downward before it can bear fruit upward. J. A. Bengle says that novices usually have "an abundance of verdure (vegetation)" and are "not yet pruned by the cross." In 1 Timothy 3:10, referring to qualifications for deacons, Paul urges, "They must first be tested."

The church in Ephesus was a decade old when Timothy became its pastor. This church had in it a galaxy of gifted teachers, so there were many men of mature experience in it; hence Paul's insistence that the new minister be mature—not as old as the others but as spiritually rooted and fruitful. Paul did not insist on maturity as a qualification to lead the newly established church at Crete (Titus 1:5–9), where mature members were not yet present. In the early stages of building a church, we cannot insist on maturity, but every care must be taken that those developing the work be stable in character, spiritual in outlook, and not ambitious for position.

Paul warns that a person not ready for leadership, and thrust into the role, "may become conceited and fall under the same judgment as the devil" (1 Timothy 3:6). A new convert does not yet possess the spiritual stability essential to leading people wisely. It is unwise to give key positions too early even to those who demonstrate promising talent, lest status spoil them. The story of the church and its mission is filled with examples of failed leaders who were appointed too soon. A novice suddenly placed in authority over others faces the danger of inflated ego. Instead, the promising convert should be given a widening opportunity to serve at humbler and less prominent tasks that will develop both natural and spiritual gifts. He should not be advanced too fast, lest he become puffed up. Neither should he be repressed, lest he become discouraged.

Paul did not appoint elders in every place on his first missionary journey. He sometimes waited until a later visit when questions about spiritual development had been clarified by time and experience (Acts 14:23). Timothy was converted during Paul's first journey, but not ordained until the second journey.[4]

"It is the mark of a grown-up man, as compared with a callow youth, that he finds his center of gravity wherever he happens to be at the moment, and however much he longs for the object of his desire, it cannot prevent him from staying at his post and doing his duty," wrote Dietrich Bonhoeffer. That is just what a new convert finds difficult to do. Steadfastness is a characteristic that accompanies a growing maturity and stability.

Maturity is shown in a magnanimous spirit and broad vision. Paul's encounter with Christ transformed him from a narrow-minded bigot into a full-hearted leader. The indwelling Christ enlarged his passion for others, broadened his view of the world, and deepened his convictions. But even in Paul's case, these changes took time.

The importance of the above requirements for leadership in the Christian church are recognized even in secular circles. The pagan Onosander described the ideal field commander: "He must be prudently self-controlled, sober, frugal, enduring in toil, intelligent, without love of money, neither young nor old, if possible the father of a family, able to speak competently, and of good reputation."[5]

If the world demands such standards of its leaders, the church of the living God should select its leaders with even greater care.

FOR REFLECTION

A. For the apostle Paul, time and experience were tools God used to prepare leaders. How long have you been aware that God has you in spiritual leadership training?

B. Which of the training areas mentioned in this chapter (social, moral, mental, personality, domestic, and maturity) has God been emphasizing recently? In what ways?

C. "Paul," this chapter declares, "had boundless, Christ-centered ambition." How would you describe the level of Christ-centered ambition in your life? In what areas does it express itself most clearly?

7

INSIGHTS ON LEADERSHIP FROM PETER

To the elders among you, I appeal as a fellow elder, a witness to Christ's sufferings and one who will also share in the glory to be revealed: Be shepherds of God's flock that is under your care, serving as overseers—not because you must, but because you are willing, as God wants you to be; not greedy for money, but eager to serve; not lording it over those entrusted to you, but being examples to the flock. And when the Chief Shepherd appears, you will receive the crown of glory that will never fade away.

Young men, in the same way be submissive to those who are older. All of you, clothe yourselves with humility toward one another, because, "God opposes the proud, but gives grace to the humble."

Humble yourselves, therefore, under God's mighty hand, that he may lift you up in due time. Cast all your anxiety on him because he cares for you.

1 Peter 5:1–7

Peter was the natural leader of the apostolic band. What Peter did, the others did; where he went, the others went. His mistakes, which sprang from his impetuous personality, were many, but his influence and leadership were without equal. We do well to ponder the advice of Peter's mature years to spiritual leaders of every generation.

See that your "flock of God" is properly fed and cared for, Peter urges (1 Peter 5:2). Such is a shepherd's primary responsibility. In these words we can hear the resonance of Peter's never-to-be-forgotten interview with Jesus after his failure, the conversation that restored him and assured him of Jesus' continuing love and care (John 21:15–22). Likewise, these "strangers in the world" (1 Peter 1:1) about whom

Peter was writing were themselves passing through deep trials. Peter could feel for them and with them, and he wrote his letter to elders with that in mind.

Peter does not approach his readers from above, as a virtuoso apostle. Rather, he takes the position of fellow elder, alongside the others, bearing similar burdens. He also writes as a witness to the sufferings of Christ, one whose heart has been humbled by failure, broken and conquered by Calvary's love. He is a leader who looks across at others but not down. A shepherd's work requires a shepherd's heart.

First, Peter deals with a leader's motivation. The spiritual leader is to approach the work willingly, not by coercion. Leaders of the church in Peter's day faced challenges that would daunt the stoutest heart, yet Peter urges that they not faint or retreat from them. Nor should leaders serve from a sense of mere duty but because of love. The work of pastoring and helping new believers is to be done "as God wants," not directed by personal preferences or desires. Barclay captures the spirit of Peter's plea:

> Peter says to the leaders, "Shepherd your people like God." Our whole attitude to the people we serve must be the attitude of God. What a vision opens out! What an ideal! It is our task to show people the forbearance of God, the forgiveness of God, the seeking love of God, the limitless service of God.[1]

When God calls us, we cannot refuse from a sense of inadequacy. Nobody is worthy of such trust. When Moses tried that excuse, God became angry (Exodus 4:14). Let us not pass the buck of leadership because we think ourselves incapable.

The spiritual leader cannot have money in his eyes when service beckons. Do not work as one "greedy for money," Peter warns (1 Peter 5:2). Perhaps Peter had in mind Judas, whose passion for money led to his fall. Leaders will be called upon to formulate policy, to set budgets and decide priorities, to deal with property. None of that can be done well if personal gain looms as a background motive.

Paul Rees suggests that the greed Peter warns against extends beyond money to fame and prestige, which are sometimes a more insidious temptation. Whether for fame or fortune, avarice cannot coexist with leadership in the church.[2]

"I am not sure which of the two occupies the lower sphere, he who hungers for money or he who thirsts for applause," wrote J. H. Jowett. "A preacher may dress and smooth his message to court the public cheers, and laborers in other spheres may bid for prominence, for imposing print, for grateful recognition. All this unfits us for our task. It destroys perception of the needs and perils of the sheep."[3]

The Christian leader must not be dictatorial. "Not lording it over those entrusted to you" (1 Peter 5:3). A domineering manner, an unbridled ambition, an offensive strut, a tyrant's talk—no attitude could be less fit for one who claims to be a servant of the Son of God.

A leader must be a worthy example for the people. "But being examples to the flock" (1 Peter 5:3). These words remind us of Paul's advice to Timothy: "But set an example for the believers in speech, in life, in love, faith and in purity" (1 Timothy 4:12). Peter teaches that elders need the shepherd spirit. Should elders ever forget whose flock they lead, Peter reminds them that it is God's. Jesus is the chief shepherd; we are assistants and associates working under His authority.

If done "as God wants," then leadership will surely include intercessory prayer. The saintly Bishop Azariah of India once remarked to Bishop Stephen Neill that he found time to pray daily, by name, for every leader in his extensive diocese. Little wonder that during his thirty years of eldering there, the diocese tripled its membership and greatly increased in spiritual effectiveness.[4]

The leader must be clothed "with humility" (1 Peter 5:5). The verb refers to a slave's tying on a white apron, which gives this verse an added note of meaning. Was Peter recalling the sad night when he refused to take the towel and wash his master's feet? Would pride keep other leaders from joyful service? Pride ever lurks at the heels of power, but God will not encourage proud men in His service. Rather, He will oppose and obstruct them. But to the undershepherd who is humble and lowly in heart, God will add power and grace to the work. In verse 5, Peter urged leaders to act humbly in relating to others. But in verse 6 he challenges leaders to react humbly to the discipline of God. "Therefore humbly submit to God's strong hand" is Charles B. Williams's rendering.

Peter concludes this section of teaching with a mention of heavenly reward: "When the Chief Shepherd appears, you will receive the crown of glory that will not fade away" (1 Peter 5:4). An athlete's crown would wither; even a king's crown would rust. But no such loss comes to the Christian servant who has chosen treasures in heaven to comforts on earth.

Are we alone in the leader's role? Do we work in solitude? Not at all, Peter announces. Rather, our frustrations and worries are shared with God, who offers relief and reprieve. "Cast all your anxiety on him because he cares for you" (1 Peter 5:7). The Christian leader need not fear that care of the flock of God will be too heavy a burden. By God's invitation, the leader can transfer the weight of spiritual burdens onto shoulders bigger, stronger, broader, and durable. God cares for you. Let worries go!

FOR REFLECTION:

A. In what ways does the statement on page 48, "Let us not pass the buck of leadership because we think ourselves incapable," affect your thinking about accepting a leadership role?

B. Peter's teaching reveals he learned a lot from negative experiences (watching Judas operate—see page 48—or remembering his own failures and Christ's restoration). What have you learned about leadership from your own mistakes?

C. How much is the discomfort or dread of standing alone shaping your view of leadership or your present role as a leader?

8

ESSENTIAL
QUALITIES OF
LEADERSHIP

Now the overseer must be above reproach, the husband of but one wife, temperate,
self-controlled, respectable, hospitable, able to teach, not given to drunkenness,
not violent but gentle, not quarrelsome, not a lover of money.

He must manage his own family well and see that his children obey him with proper
respect. (If anyone does not know how to manage his own family, how can he take care
of God's church?) He must not be a recent convert, or he may become conceited, and fall
under the same judgment as the devil. He must also have a good reputation with
outsiders, so that he will not fall into disgrace and into the devil's trap.

1 Timothy 3:2–7

Jesus trained His disciples superbly for their future roles. He taught by example and by precept; His teaching was done "on the road." Jesus did not ask the Twelve to sit down and take notes in a formal classroom. Jesus' classrooms were the highways of life; His principles and values came across in the midst of daily experience. Jesus placed disciples into internships (Luke 10:17–24) that enabled them to learn through failure and success (Mark 9:14–29). He delegated authority and responsibility to them as they were able to bear it. Jesus' wonderful teaching in John 13–16 was their graduation address.

God prepares leaders with a specific place and task in mind. Training methods are adapted to the mission, and natural and spiritual gifts are given with clear purpose. An example is Paul, who never could have accomplished so much without directed training and divine endowment.

Similarly, God prepared Adoniram Judson to become a missionary pioneer in Burma by giving to this remarkable leader qualities necessary for launching the gospel in the Indian subcontinent—self-reliance balanced by humility, energy restrained by prudence, self-forgetfulness, courage, and a passion for souls.

Martin Luther has been described as a man easy to approach, without personal vanity, and so plain in his tastes that people wondered how he could find any pleasure with so little money. He had common sense, a playful humor, eager laughter, sincerity, and honesty. Add to those qualities his courage, conviction, and passion for Christ. It is no wonder that he inspired loyalty in others that had the strength of steel.[1]

Professor G. Warneck described Hudson Taylor, the missionary pioneer to China: "A man full of faith and the Holy Ghost, of entire surrender to God and His call, of great self-denial, heartfelt compassion, rare poser in prayer, marvelous organizing faculty, indefatigable perseverance, and of astounding influence with men, and withal of childlike simplicity himself."[2]

God gave these leaders gifts and talents that fit the mission to which they were called. What raised these men above their fellows was the degree to which they developed those gifts through devotion and discipline.

Discipline
Without this essential quality, all other gifts remain as dwarfs: they cannot grow. So discipline appears first on our list. Before we can conquer the world, we must first conquer the self.

A leader is a person who has learned to obey a discipline imposed from without, and has then taken on a more rigorous discipline from within. Those who rebel against authority and scorn self-discipline—who shirk the rigors and turn from the sacrifices—do not qualify to lead. Many who drop out of ministry are sufficiently gifted, but have large areas of life floating free from the Holy Spirit's control. Lazy and disorganized people never rise to true leadership.

Many who aspire to leadership fail because they have never learned to follow. They are like boys playing war in the street, but all is quiet. When you ask, "Is there a truce?" they respond, "No, we are all generals. No one will obey the command to charge."

Donald Barnhouse noted with interest that the average age of the 40,000 people listed in *Who's Who in America*—the people who run the country—was under twenty-eight. Discipline in early life, which is ready to make sacrifices in order to gain adequate preparation for life tasks, paves the way for high achievement.[3]

A great statesman made a speech that turned the tide of national affairs. "May I ask how long you spent preparing that speech?" asked an admirer.

"All my life," he replied.

The young man of leadership caliber will work while others waste time, study while others snooze, pray while others daydream. Slothful habits are overcome, whether in thought, deed, or dress. The emerging leader eats right, stands tall, and prepares himself to wage spiritual warfare. He will without reluctance undertake the unpleasant task that others avoid or the hidden duty that others evade because it wins no public applause. As the Spirit fills his life, he learns not to shrink from difficult situations or retreat from hard-edged people. He will kindly and courageously administer rebuke when that is called for, or he will exercise the necessary discipline when the interests of the Lord's work demand it. He will not procrastinate, but will prefer to dispatch with the hardest tasks first. His persistent prayer will be:

> *God, harden me against myself,*
> *The coward with pathetic voice*
> *Who craves for ease and rest and joy.*
> *Myself, arch-traitor to myself,*
> *My hollowest friend,*
> *My deadliest foe,*
> *My clog, whatever road I go.*[4]

Few men were more faithful and courageous in giving loving rebuke or speaking frankly to people than Fred Mitchell, British director of the China Inland Mission and chairman of the English Keswick Convention. Sensitive and affectionate, he did not turn from the unpleasant interview. He always spoke in love, after much prayer. But his words did not always fall on receptive ears. He confided how much he had suffered when his faithfulness to God's work led to the loss of a friend. As he reached older age, Fred spent even more time praying before speaking. Often when he needed to deal with a matter of discipline, he would write a letter, then keep it for several days. Sometimes, on rereading it, he was assured it was right to send it, so it would be mailed. Sometimes he destroyed the draft and wrote another.[5]

When the founder of the World Dominion Movement, Thomas Cochrane, was interviewed for the mission field, he faced this question: "To what position of the field do you feel specially called?" He answered, "I only know I should wish it to be the hardest you could offer me"—the reply of a disciplined person.

Lytton Strachey described Florence Nightingale:

> *It was not by gentle sweetness and womanly self-abnegation that she brought order out of chaos in the Scutari hospitals, that from her own resources she had clothed the British Army, that she had spread her dominion over the serried and reluctant powers of the official world; it was by strict method, by stern discipline, by rigid attention to detail, by ceaseless labor, by the fixed determination of an indomitable will. Beneath her cool and calm demeanor, there lurked fierce and passionate fires.[6]*

Samuel Chadwick, the great Methodist preacher and principal of Cliff College, made an immense impact on his generation. He rose at six each morning and took a cold bath, summer and winter. His study light was seldom out before two in the morning. That rigorous lifestyle was the outward expression of his intense inner discipline.[7]

Throughout his life, George Whitefield rose at four in the morning and retired each night at ten. When that hour struck, he would rise from his seat, no matter who his visitors or what the conversation, and say good-naturedly to his friends, "Come, gentlemen, it is time for all good folks to be at home."[8]

> *Barclay Buxton of Japan would urge Christians to lead disciplined lives whether they were in business or evangelistic*

*work. This included disciplined Bible study and prayer, tithing,
use of time, keeping healthy with proper diet, sleep, and
exercise. It included the rigor of disciplined fellowship among
Christians who differed from each other in many ways.*[9]

These glimpses of personal biography illustrate the meaning of an
unknown poet:

> *The heights by great men reached and kept
> Were not attained by sudden flight;
> But they, while their companions slept,
> Were toiling upward in the night.*

If a leader shows strong discipline, others will see it and cooperate with the expectations placed on them. At this point, leadership by
example is crucial.

There is another element in discipline that receives too little attention. We must be willing to receive from others as well as give to others. Some sacrificial souls delight in sacrificing themselves, but refuse
reciprocal gestures. They do not want to feel obligated to those they
are serving. But real leadership recognizes the value of the gestures of
others. To neglect receiving kindness and help is to isolate oneself, to
rob others of opportunity, and to deprive oneself of sustenance. Our
example in this is the ultimate Servant Jesus, who came to serve but
graciously accepted the service of others—people like His hosts Mary
and Martha, the use of the colt He rode into Jerusalem, and others.

Bishop Westcott admitted at the end of his life to one great mistake.
He had always helped others, but just as rigorously he had resisted
others serving him. As a result, his life had an empty spot where sweet
friendship and human care might have been.[10]

Vision

Those who have most powerfully and permanently influenced their
generation have been "seers"—people who have seen more and farther
than others—persons of faith, for faith is vision. Moses, one of the

great leaders of all history, "endured as seeing him who is invisible." His faith imparted vision. Elisha's servant saw the obvious menace of the encircling army, but Elisha saw the vast invisible hosts of heaven. His faith imparted vision.

Powhatten James wrote:

> *The man of God must have insight into things spiritual. He must be able to see the mountains filled with the horses and chariots of fire; he must be able to interpret that which is written by the finger of God upon the walls of conscience; he must be able to translate the signs of the times into terms of their spiritual meaning: he must be able to draw aside, now and then, the curtain of things material and let mortals glimpse the spiritual glories which crown the mercy seat of God. The man of God must declare the pattern that was shown him on the mount; he must utter the vision granted to him upon the isle of revelation. . . . None of these things can he do without spiritual insight.*[11]

Charles Cowman, founder of the Oriental Missionary Society, was "a man of vision. Throughout his life he seemed to see what the crowd did not see, and to see wider and fuller than many of his own day. He was man of far horizons."[12]

Vision involves foresight as well as insight. President McKinley's reputation for greatness rested in part on his ability to put an ear to the ground and listen for things coming. He turned his listening into vision; he saw what lay ahead. A leader must be able to see the end results of the policies and methods he or she advocates. Responsible leadership always looks ahead to see how policies will affect future generations.

The great missionary pioneers were people of vision. Carey saw the whole globe while fellow preachers limited the world to their parish borders. Henry Martyn saw India, Persia, and Arabia—the Muslim world—while the church at home squabbled over petty theological disagreements. People said of A. B. Simpson: "His lifework seemed to be to push on alone, where his fellows had seen nothing to explore."

A senior colleague once told Douglas Thornton of Egypt: "Thornton, you are different from anyone else I know. You are always looking at the end of things. Most people, myself included, find it better to do the next thing." Thornton's answer: "I find that the constant inspiration gained by looking at the goal is the chief thing that helps me to persevere."[13] An ideal, a vision, was absolutely necessary to him. He could not work without it. And that explained the largeness of his views and the magnitude of his schemes.

Eyes that look are common; eyes that see are rare. The Pharisees *looked at* Peter and saw only an unschooled fisherman—not worth a second look. Jesus *saw in* Peter a prophet and preacher, saint and leader who would help turn the world upside down.

Vision involves optimism and hope. The pessimist sees difficulty in every opportunity. The optimist sees opportunity in every difficulty. The pessimist tends to hold back people of vision from pushing ahead. Caution has its role to play. We all live in a real world of limitation and inertia. Cautious Christians draw valuable lessons from history and tradition, but are in danger of being chained to the past. The person who sees the difficulties so clearly that he does not discern the possibilities cannot inspire a vision in others.

Browning described the courageous optimist:

> *One who has never turned his back,*
> *But marched breast-forward,*
> *Never doubting clouds would break,*
> *Never dreamed, though right were worsted,*
> *Wrong would triumph.*

Vision leads to venture, and history is on the side of venturesome faith. The person of vision takes fresh steps of faith across gullies and chasms, not "playing safe" but neither taking foolish risks. Concerning Archbishop Mowll it is written:

> *It was a mark of his greatness that he was never behind his*
> *age, or too far ahead. He was up at the front, and far enough*

in advance to lead the march. He was always catching sight of
new horizons. He still had a receptive mind for new ideas at an
age when many were inclined to let things take their course.[14]

Leaders take lessons from the past, but never sacrifice the future for
the sake of mere continuity. People of vision gauge decisions on the
future; the story of the past cannot be rewritten.

> *A vision without a task makes a visionary.*
> *A task without a vision is drudgery.*
> *A vision with a task makes a missionary.*[15]

Wisdom

"Wisdom is the faculty of making the use of knowledge, a com-
bination of discernment, judgment, sagacity, and similar powers. . .
. In Scripture, right judgment concerning spiritual and moral truth"
(Webster).

If knowledge is the accumulation of facts and intelligence the development of reason, wisdom is heavenly discernment. It is insight into
the heart of things. Wisdom involves knowing God and the subtleties
of the human heart. More than knowledge, it is the right application
of knowledge in moral and spiritual matters, in handling dilemmas,
in negotiating complex relationships. "Wisdom is nine-tenths a matter
of being wise in time," said Theodore Roosevelt. Most of us are "too
often wise after the event."[16]

Wisdom gives a leader balance and helps to avoid eccentricity and
extravagance. If knowledge comes by study, wisdom comes by Holy
Spirit filling. Then a leader can apply knowledge correctly. "Full of
wisdom" is one of the requirements for even subordinate leaders in
the early church (Acts 6:3).

> *Knowledge and wisdom, far from being one,*
> *Have ofttimes no connection. Knowledge dwells*
> *In heads replete with thoughts of other men:*
> *Wisdom, in minds attentive to their own.*

Knowledge is proud that he has learned so much,
Wisdom is humble, that he knows no more.

Author unknown

D. E. Hoste knew the importance of wisdom for leaders:

When a person in authority demands obedience of another,
irrespective of the latter's reason and conscience, this is
tyranny. On the other hand, when, by the exercise of tact and
sympathy, prayer, spiritual power and sound wisdom, one is
able to influence and enlighten another, so that a life course is
changed, that is spiritual leadership.[17]

Paul's prayer for the Christians at Colosse should always be on our lips: That "God fill you with the knowledge of his will through all spiritual wisdom and understanding" (Colossians 1:9).

Decision

When all the facts are in, swift and clear decision is another mark of a true leader. A visionary may see, but a leader must decide. An impulsive person may be quick to declare a preference; but a leader must weigh evidence and make his decision on sound premises.

Once sure of the will of God, a spiritual leader springs into action, without regard to consequences. Pursuing the goal, the leader never looks back or calculates escape strategies if plans turn sour. Nor does a true leader cast blame for failure on subordinates.

Abraham showed swift and clear decisiveness during the crisis in Canaan and the rescue of Lot (Genesis 14). In his relations with his nephew, Abraham showed both the active and passive sides of spirituality. In his unselfish yielding of his right to the choice of pasturelands (Genesis 13), Abraham displayed the passive graces of godliness. But when Lot was captured during a battle at Sodom, Abraham took immediate action. With great bravery he pursued the enemy and gained a victory over superior numbers. This is true faith.

Moses became the leader of Israel when he abandoned Egypt's power and privilege and identified with the Hebrew slaves and their suffering (Hebrews 11:24–27). These were momentous decisions. This is true faith.

Paul's first question after his dramatic conversion was "What shall I do, Lord?" (Acts 22:10). Without hesitation Paul acted on his new knowledge of Christ's deity. To be granted light was to follow it. To see duty was to do it.

The catalog of saints in Hebrews 11 is a study of vision and decision. They saw the vision, counted the cost, made their decisions, and went into action. The same sequence is evident in the lives of great missionary leaders. Carey saw the vision in Kettering and made his decision for India, though the difficulties of getting there loomed as high as heaven itself. Livingstone saw the vision in Dumbarton, made his decision, overcame all obstacles, and proceeded to Africa.[18] Circumstances cannot frustrate such people, or difficulties deter them.

The spiritual leader will not procrastinate when faced with a decision, nor vacillate after making it. A sincere but faulty decision is better than weak-willed "trial balloons" or indecisive overtures. To postpone decision is really to decide for the status quo. In most decisions the key element is not so much knowing what to do but in living with the results.

Charles Cowman had the reputation of being a man of purpose. His eyes were fixed on one great object. With him, a vision was the first step in an action plan. The moment he sensed a possibility, he was uneasy until achievement was underway.

A young man beginning his work with the Coast Guard was called with his crew to try a desperate rescue in a great storm. Frightened, rain and wind pounding his face, the man cried to his captain, "We will never get back!" The captain replied, "We don't have to come back, but we must go out."

Courage

Leaders require courage of the highest order—always moral courage and often physical courage as well. Courage is that quality of mind that enables people to encounter danger or difficulty firmly, without fear or discouragement.

Paul admitted to knowing fear, but it never stopped him. "I came to you in weakness and fear, and with much trembling," he reported in 1 Corinthians 2:3, but the verb is *came*. He did not stay home out of fear for the journey. In 2 Corinthians 7:5, Paul confesses "conflicts on the outside, fears within." He did not court danger but never let it keep him from the Master's work.

Martin Luther was among the most fearless men who ever lived.[19] When he set out on his journey to Worms to face the questions and the controversies his teaching had created, he said, "You can expect from me everything save fear or recantation. I shall not flee, much less recant." His friends warned of the dangers; some begged him not to go. But Luther would not hear of it. "Not go to Worms!" he said. "I shall go to Worms though there were as many devils as tiles on the roofs."[20]

When Luther appeared there before the court of Emperor Charles V, he was shown a stack of his writings and called upon to recant. Luther replied, "Unless I can be instructed and convinced with evidence from the Holy Scriptures or with open, clear, and distinct grounds of reasoning, then I cannot and will not recant, because it is neither safe nor wise to act against conscience."

Then he likely added: "Here I stand. I can do no other. God help me! Amen."

A few days before his death, Luther recalled that day. "I was afraid of nothing: God can make one so desperately bold."

Not everyone is courageous by nature. Some people are more naturally timid than Luther. But whether we are bold or reticent, God calls leaders to be of good courage and not to capitulate to fear. Such a call to courage would be rather pointless if nobody feared anything. Because fear is a real part of life, God gives us the Holy Spirit, who fills us with power. But we must let that power do its work, and not fear.

Consider these two contrasting statements: "The doors were locked for fear of the Jews" (John 20:19), and, "When they saw the courage of Peter and John" (Acts 4:13). These statements describe the same disciples, and the same opposition. The difference is time. What happened between the first and the second? The Holy Spirit gave "not a spirit of timidity, but a spirit of power" (2 Timothy 1:7).

Courageous leaders face unpleasant and even devastating situations with equanimity, then act firmly to bring good from trouble, even if their action is unpopular. Leadership always faces natural human inertia and opposition. But courage follows through with a task until it is done.

People expect leaders to be calm and courageous during a crisis. While others lose their heads, leaders stay the course. Leaders strengthen followers in the middle of discouraging setbacks and shattering reverses.

Facing the ruthless armies of Sennacherib, Hezekiah made his military preparations and then set about strengthening the morale of his people. "Be strong and courageous," he told them. "Do not be afraid or discouraged because of the king of Assyria and the vast army with him. . . . With him is only the arm of flesh, but with us is the LORD our God to help us and to fight our battles." And then the Scriptures report that "the people gained confidence from what Hezekiah the king of Judah said" (2 Chronicles 32:7–8). Here is leadership, active and strong.

Humility

Humility is also a hallmark of the spiritual leader. Christ told His disciples to turn away from the pompous attitudes of the oriental despots, and instead take on the lowly bearing of the servant (Matthew 20:25–27). As in ancient days, so today humility is least admired in political and business circles. But no bother! The spiritual leader will choose the hidden path of sacrificial service and approval of the Lord over the flamboyant self-advertising of the world.

We often regard John the Baptist as great because of his burning eloquence and blistering denunciation of the evils of his day. His words pierced and exposed the hearts of many a petty ruler. But his real greatness was revealed in one infinitely wise affirmation: "He must increase, but I must decrease" (John 3:30). Here John's spiritual stature rings clear and strong.

A leader's humility should grow with the passing of years, like other attitudes and qualities. Notice Paul's advance in the grace of humility. Early in his ministry, he acknowledged: "I am the least of the apostles and do not deserve to be called an apostle" (1 Corinthians 15:9). Later he volunteered: "I am less than the least of all God's people" (Ephesians 3:8). Toward the end of his life, he spoke of the mercies of Christ and his own sense of place: "Christ Jesus came into the world to save sinners—of whom I am the worst" (1 Timothy 1:15).

William Law writes in his devotional classic *Serious Call*:

> *Let every day be a day of humility; condescend to all the weaknesses and infirmities of your fellow-creature, cover their frailties, love their excellencies, encourage their virtues, relieve their wants, rejoice in their prosperities, compassionate over their distress, receive their friendship, overlook the unkindness, forgive their malice, be a servant of servants, and condescend to do the lowliest offices of the lowest of mankind.*[21]

On one occasion when Samuel Brengle was introduced as "the great Doctor Brengle," he noted in his diary:

> *If I appear great in their eyes, the Lord is most graciously helping me to see how absolutely nothing I am without Him, and helping me to keep little in my own eyes. He does use me. But I am so concerned that He uses me and that it is not of me the work is done. The axe cannot boast of the trees it has cut down. It could do nothing but for the woodsman. He made it, he sharpened it, and he used it. The moment he throws it aside; it becomes only old iron. O that I may never lose sight of this."*[22]

The spiritual leader of today is the one who gladly worked as an assistant and associate, humbly helping another achieve great things. Robert Morrison of China wrote: "The great fault in our missions is that no one likes to be second."[23]

Integrity and Sincerity

Paul spoke of his failures and successes with an openness few of us are prepared to copy. Even before his conversion he served God sincerely

(2 Timothy 1:3) and with great personal integrity. Later he wrote: "In Christ we speak before God with sincerity" (2 Corinthians 2:17).

These two qualities of leadership were part of God's law for the Israelites (Deuteronomy 18:13). God wants His people to show a transparent character, open and innocent of guile.

A prominent businessman once replied to a question: "If I had to name the one most important quality of a top manager, I would say, personal integrity." Surely the spiritual leader must be sincere in promise, faithful in discharge of duty, upright in finances, loyal in service, and honest in speech.

FOR REFLECTION

    A. This chapter describes eight essential qualities of leadership: discipline, vision, wisdom, decision, courage, humility, integrity, and sincerity. Which one needs the most attention in your life right now? Why?

    B. How would you explain the point that discipline has an effect on the development of every other leadership quality?

    C. Describe the difference between integrity and sincerity as you understand these spiritual qualities.

9
MORE ESSENTIAL QUALITIES OF LEADERSHIP

Deacons, likewise, are to be men worthy of respect, sincere, not indulging in much wine, and not pursuing dishonest gain. They must keep hold of the deep truths of the faith with a clear conscience. They must first be tested; and if there is nothing against them, let them serve as deacons.

1 Timothy 3:8–10

Humor

Our sense of humor is a gift from God that should be controlled as well as cultivated. Clean, wholesome humor will relax tension and relieve difficult situations. Leaders can use it to displace tension with a sense of the normal.

Samuel Johnson advised that people should spend part of each day laughing. Archbishop Whately, the great apologist, wrote: "We ought not only to cultivate the cornfield of the mind but the pleasure grounds also." Agnes Strickland claimed that "next to virtue, the fun in this world is what we can least spare."[1]

Criticized for including humor in a sermon, Charles Spurgeon, eye twinkling, said: "If only you knew how much I hold back, you would commend me." Later writing on the subject, he said: "There are things in these sermons that may produce smiles, but what of them? The preacher is not quite sure about a smile being a sin, and at any rate he thinks it less a crime to cause a momentary laughter than a half-hour of profound slumber."

Helmut Thielecke wrote:

> *Should we not see that lines of laughter about the eyes are just
> as much marks of faith as are the lines of care and seriousness?
> Is it only earnestness that is baptized? Is laughter pagan? . . .
> A church is in a bad way when it banishes laughter from the
> sanctuary and leaves it to the cabaret, the nightclub and the
> toastmasters.*[2]

Humor is a great asset and an invaluable lubricant in missionary
life. Indeed it is a most serious deficiency if a missionary lacks a sense
of humor. A Swede was urged by friends to give up the idea of return-
ing to India as a missionary because it was so hot there. "Man," he was
urged, "it is 120 degrees in the shade!"

"Vell," said the Swede in noble contempt, "ve don't always have to
stay in the shade, do ve?"

A. E. Norrish, a missionary to India, testified:

> *I have never met leadership without a sense of humor; this
> ability to stand outside oneself and one's circumstances, to see
> things in perspective and laugh. It is a great safety value! You
> will never lead others far without the joy of the Lord and its
> concomitant, a sense of humor.*[3]

Douglas Thornton was often more amusing than he tried to be. He
had a delightful way of mixing up two kindred proverbs or idioms.
Once he told his companions that he always had two strings up his
sleeve. They then asked him if he also had another card to his bow.
Such exchanges enliven heavy committee meetings and create wholesome laughter.

After a half century of ministry, F. J. Hallett claimed that in the actual
work of a parish, the most successful leader is the one who possesses a
keen sense of humor combined with a clear sense of God's grace. The
humor lends pungency, originality, and eloquence to sermons.

Of one great preacher it was said that he used humor as a condi-
ment and a stimulant. At times, paroxysms of laugher would rock his

audience—never about sacred matters. Following the joke, he would quickly swing to the sublime. His humor never fell into frivolity.

A good test of the appropriateness of a joke is whether the humor controls us or we control it. About Kenneth Strachan, general director of the Latin American Mission, it was said: "He had a keen sense of humor, but he had a sense of the fitness of things. He knew the place for a joke and his humor was controlled."[4]

Anger

Can this be right? An angry leader? Indeed, Jesus had this quality, and when we use it rightly, we follow Him. In Mark 3:5, Jesus looked "at them with anger." The Pharisees had just given Him a stubborn, silent answer to a question, so He gave them an equally silent rebuke.

Holy anger has its roots in genuine love. Both are part of the nature of God. Jesus' love for the man with the withered hand aroused His anger against those who would deny him healing. Jesus' love for God's house made Him angry at the sellers and buyers who had turned the temple into a "den of robbers" (Matthew 21:13). Yet in both these cases and others, it was ultimately Jesus' love for those doing wrong that caused Him to be angry with them. His anger got their attention!

Great leaders—people who turn the tide and change the direction of events—have been angry at injustice and abuse that dishonors God and enslaves the weak. William Wilberforce moved heaven and earth to emancipate slaves in England and eliminate the slave trade—and he was angry!

F. W. Robertson described his sense of anger on one special occasion: "My blood was at the moment running fire, and I remembered that once in my life I had felt a terrible might; I knew and rejoiced to know that I was inflicting the sentence of a coward's and a liar's hell."[5] Martin Luther claimed that he "never did anything well until his wrath was excited, and then he could do anything well."

But holy anger is open to abuse. Many who feel it allow anger to become their downfall. It can all too easily become a preferred response even when other responses would be more effective. Bishop Butler teaches six conditions that make anger sinful:

- *When, to favor a resentment or feud, we imagine an injury done to us*
- *When an injury done to us becomes, in our minds, greater than it really is*
- *When, without real injury, we feel resentment on account of pain or inconvenience*
- *When indignation rises too high, and overwhelms our ability to restrain*
- *When we gratify resentments by causing pain or harm out of revenge*
- *When we are so perplexed and angry at sin in our own lives that we readily project anger at the sin we find in others.*[6]

Paul argues for holy anger when he repeats the advice of Psalm 4:4: "In your anger do not sin" (Ephesians 4:26). This anger is not selfish and does not center on the pain you currently feel. To be free of sin such anger must be zealous for truth and purity, with the glory of God its chief objective.

> *Thou to wax fierce*
> *In the cause of the Lord!*
> *Anger and zeal*
> *And the joy of the brave,*
> *Who bade thee to feel,*
> *Sin's slave?*

Author unknown

Patience

Spiritual leaders need a healthy endowment of patience. Chrysostom called patience the queen of virtues. Often we think of patience in passive terms, as if the patient person is utterly submissive and half asleep. But this version of patience needs a biblical corrective. Barclay teaches from 2 Peter 1:6 (where the King James Version uses the term *patience*):

The word never means the spirit which sits with folded
hands and simply bears things. It is victorious endurance . . .
Christian steadfastness, the brave and courageous acceptance
of everything life can do to us, and the transmuting of even the
worst into another step on the upward way. It is the courageous
and triumphant ability to bear things, which enables a man to
pass breaking point and not to break, and always to greet the
unseen with a cheer.[7]

Patience meets its most difficult test in personal relationships. Paul lost his patience dealing with John Mark. Hudson Taylor once confessed: "My greatest temptation is to lose my temper over the slackness and inefficiency so disappointing in those on whom I depend. It is no use to lose my temper—only kindness. But oh, it is such a trial."[8]

Many leaders can identify with Taylor's struggle. But in the face of doubting Thomas, the unstable Peter, and traitorous Judas, how marvelous was the patience of our Lord!

A leader shows patience by not running too far ahead of his followers and thus discouraging them. While keeping ahead, he stays near enough for them to keep him in sight and hear his call forward. He is not so strong that he cannot show strengthening sympathy for the weakness of his fellow travelers. "We who are strong ought to bear with the failings of the weak," Paul wrote in Romans 15:1.

The person who is impatient with weakness will be ineffective in his leadership. The evidence of our strength lies not in the distance that separates us from other runners but in our closure with them, our slower pace for their sakes, our helping them pick it up and cross the line.

Ernest Gordon described his father, A. J. Gordon, with these words: "Criticism and opposition he endured without recrimination."[9]

When we lead by persuasion rather than command, patience is essential. Leaders rightly cultivate the art of persuasion that allows maximum individual decision making and ownership of a plan. Often, a leader's plan of action must wait for collegial support—ever patient—until the team is ready. D. E. Hoste remembered a great leader:

I shall never forget the impression made upon me by Hudson
Taylor in connection with these affairs. Again and again he was
obliged either to greatly modify or lay aside projects which were
sound and helpful but met with determined opposition. . . .
Later, in answer to patient continuance in prayer, many of
[these] projects were [put into] effect. [10]

Friendship

You can measure leaders by the number and quality of their friends.
Judged by that measuring rod, Paul had a genius for friendship. He
was essentially a gregarious man. His relationship with Timothy was a
model of friendship between generations; Paul and Luke are a model
between contemporaries.

A. B. Simpson earned this sterling tribute: "The crowning glory of his
leadership was that he was a friend of man. He loved the man next to
him and he loved mankind." [11] David's leadership sprang from his genius
at gathering around him men of renown who were ready to die for him.
So fully did he capture their affection and allegiance that a casual wish
was to them a command (2 Samuel 23:15). They were prepared to die
for him, because they knew David was fully ready to die for them.

The apostle Paul similarly had loyal friends. "No man in the New
Testament made fiercer enemies than Paul, but few men in the world
had better friends. They clustered around him so thickly that we are apt
to lose their personality in their devotion." [12] Yes, Paul led his friends
into all sorts of risks for Christ's sake, but they followed him cheer-
fully, confident of his love for them. Paul's letters glow with warm
appreciation and personal affection for his fellows.

Leaders must draw the best out of people, and friendship does that
far better than prolonged argument or mere logic. John R. Mott counseled leaders to "rule by the heart. When reasons and arguments fail,
fall back on the heart-genuine friendship."

Robert A. Jaffrey played a major role in opening Vietnam to the
gospel. He did so largely because of this quality that all great leaders
share. "Nothing can take the place of affection. . . . Intellect will not

do. Bible knowledge is not enough." Jaffrey loved people for their own sakes. He was happy in the presence of human beings, whatever their race and colour.[13]

Few Christian leaders enjoy the reputation won by Charles Spurgeon, the greatest British preacher of the late nineteenth century. His biographer wrote that "he exercised an absolute authority, not because of sheer willfulness, though he was a willful man, but because of his acknowledged worth. Men bowed to his authority because it was authority backed by united wisdom and affection."

One greater than Spurgeon or David or Paul ruled His followers by friendship and affection. Of Him it was written, "Having loved his own who were in the world, he now showed them the full extent of his love" (John 13:1). Indeed, Peter confessed with broken heart in response to Jesus' enduring affection, "Lord, you know all things. You know that I love you" (John 21:17).

Tact and Diplomacy

The root meaning of "tact" has to do with touching. The tactile sense is the ability to feel through touch. Concerning relationships, tact is the ability to deal with people sensitively, to avoid giving offense, to have a "feel" for the proper words or responses to a delicate situation.

Diplomacy is the ability to manage delicate situations, especially involving people from different cultures, and certainly from differing opinions.

Leaders need to be able to reconcile opposing viewpoints without giving offense or compromising principle. A leader should be able to project into the life and heart and mind of another, then setting aside personal preferences, deal with the other in a fashion that fits the other best. These skills can be learned and developed.

A leader needs the ability to negotiate differences in a way that recognizes mutual rights and intelligence and yet leads to a harmonious solution. Fundamental to this skill is understanding how people feel, how people react.

Joshua used wonderful tact when he divided the Promised Land among the tribes of Israel. A wrong move would have splintered an already wobbly nation. Joshua had to be both forthright and fair. His tact beamed brightly again when the tribes of Reuben and Gad built their own altar, and thus nearly created a civil war. Joshua had wisdom learned in the school of God. His close walk with God gave him the diplomacy to steer a course away from needless bloodshed and toward national healing.

William Carey was unconsciously a diplomat. One of his fellow workers testified: "He has attained the happy art of ruling and over-ruling others without asserting his authority, or others feeling their subjection—and all is done without the least appearance of design on his part."[14]

Inspirational Power

The power of inspiring others to service and sacrifice will mark God's leader. Such a leader is like a light for others around. Charles Cowman worked hard, but he also possessed the ability to get others to work hard. His zeal and drive—and inspiration—were infectious.[15]

Pastor Hsi was one of the truly great leaders of his time in China. He too possessed this power to an extraordinary degree. A friend commented on Hsi's inspiring presence: "His power was remarkable. Without any effort, apparently, he seemed to sway everybody. Instinctively people followed and trusted him. He had great power of initiative and enterprise. You could not be with him without gaining a wholly new ideal of Christian life and service."[16]

Nehemiah had this quality. The people in Jerusalem were utterly disheartened and dispirited when he arrived. In no time he built them into an effective team of workers. Such were his powers that before long we read, "The people had a mind to work" (Nehemiah 4:6 KJV).

General Mark Clark, addressing a class of trainees, said of Winston Churchill: "I doubt if any man in history has ever made such grim utterances, yet given his people such a sense of strength, exuberance, even of cheerfulness."[17]

When France fell to the German armies and Britain was left alone in the fight, the British cabinet met in their chambers with a sense of deep gloom. When Churchill entered, he looked around at the disconsolate ministers, then said, "Gentlemen, I find this rather inspiring." Small wonder that he was able to galvanize a nation into effective counterattack.

Executive Ability

However spiritual a leader may be, he cannot translate vision into action without executive ability. It is true that subtle dangers lie in organization, for if it is overzealous it can become an unsatisfactory substitute for the working of the Holy Spirit. But lack of method and failure to organize have spelled doom for many promising ministries.

The King James Version translates Isaiah 30:18: "The Lord is a God of judgment." Here the word "judgment" means method, order, system, or law. So God is methodic and orderly. And God requires of His managers and stewards that "all things be done decently and in order." Bible commentator Sir George Smith writes: "It is a great truth that the Almighty and All-merciful is the All-methodical too. No religion is complete in its creed, or healthy in its influence, which does not insist equally on all these."[18]

Our duty is to reflect the orderliness of God in all we do for Him. Evangelism is not a matter of organizing people into the kingdom, but neither is evangelistic work justified in ignoring careful planning. We depend on the Spirit leading converts to salvation, but we also plan and act on our plans for the sake of the gospel's reach.

John Wesley had a genius for organization that is still evident in the church he founded. Because he was such a gifted executive, his movement was unshaken when death deprived it of his presence and guidance. His judgment of others, his skill in deploying them to the mission's best advantage, and to win their loyal submission amounted to genius and spared the movement from disasters that others experienced.[19]

The Therapy of Listening

To get at the root of problems, a leader must develop into a skillful listener. Too many strong personalities are compulsive talkers. "He won't listen to me," complains a missionary. "He gives the answer before I have had a chance to state the problem."

To many people, sympathetic listening is inefficient—merely waiting until someone else can state a point. But genuine listening seeks to understand another without prejudgment. A problem is often half-solved when it is clearly stated. One missionary casualty moaned: "If only he had listened to me. I needed someone to share a problem."

Leaders who want to show sensitivity should listen often and long, and talk short and seldom. Many so-called leaders are too busy to listen. True leaders know that time spent listening is well invested.

A would-be politician approached Justice Oliver Wendell Holmes for advice on how to get elected. Holmes replied: "To be able to listen to others in a sympathetic and understanding manner, is perhaps the most effective mechanism in the world for getting along with people, and tying up their friendship for good."[20]

The Art of Letter Writing

Any position of leadership involves a considerable amount of correspondence, and letters are self-revealing. Take Paul for example. We know more about his moral integrity, intellectual honesty, and spiritual life from his letters than from any other source. When a difficult situation required his attention, he dipped his pen in tears, not acid. "For I wrote to you out of great distress and anguish of heart" (2 Corinthians 2:4).

After his strong letter to the erring Corinthians, Paul's tender heart led him to wonder if he had been too severe. "Even if I caused you sorrow by my letter, I do not regret it. Though I did regret it—I see that my letter hurt you, but only for a little while. Now I am happy . . . because your sorrow led you to repentance" (2 Corinthians 7:8–9). The point of his letter was not to win an argument, but to settle a spiritual problem and produce maturity among the Christians there.

Paul's letters are filled with encouragement, were gracious in compliment, and rich in sympathy. Those who received them were always enriched (Philippians 1:27–30). But that did not restrain him from being faithful in correcting faults. "Have I now become your enemy by telling you the truth? How I wish I could be with you now and change my tone, because I am perplexed by you!" (Galatians 4:16, 20).

Clear language is important in our letters, but more important is the right spirit. For all their usefulness, letters have significant limitations as a medium of communication. They cannot smile when they are saying something difficult, and therefore additional care should be taken to see that they are warm in tone.

Letter writing formed an important part in Paul's program of instruction and follow-up. So it was for George Whitefield. It was said of him that after preaching to large crowds, he would work late into the night writing letters of encouragement to new converts.

FOR REFLECTION

A. Before reading this chapter, what importance would you have given to humor in the profile of a leader? Why?

B. How would you illustrate the effective use of anger from your experience or observations?

C. What do all the qualities described in this chapter have in common? In what aspect of a leader's life do they all function?

10
ABOVE ALL ELSE

Choose seven men from among you who are known to be full of the Spirit and wisdom. . . . They chose Stephen, a man full of faith and of the Holy Spirit.

Acts 6:3, 5

Spiritual leadership requires Spirit-filled people. Other qualities are important; to be Spirit-filled is indispensable.

The book of Acts is the story of people who established the church and led the missionary enterprise. We cannot fail to note that even the office of deacon required people "full of the Holy Spirit." These officers were to be known for integrity and judgment, but pre-eminently for their spirituality. A person can have a brilliant mind and possess artful administrative skill. But without spirituality he is incapable of giving truly spiritual leadership.

Behind all the busyness of the apostles was the executive activity of the Spirit. As supreme administrator of the church and chief strategist of the missionary enterprise, He was everywhere present. The Spirit did not delegate authority into secular or carnal hands, even when a particular job has no direct spiritual teaching involved; all workers must be Spirit-led and filled. Likewise today, selection of kingdom leaders must not be influenced by worldly wisdom, wealth, or status.

The prime consideration is spirituality. When a church or missions organization follows a different set of criteria, it essentially removes the Spirit from leadership. As a consequence, the Spirit is grieved and quenched, and the result is spiritual dearth and death for that effort.

Selecting leaders apart from spiritual qualifications leads always to unspiritual administration. A. T. Pierson compared such a situation to a large corporation that wants to oust its CEO. Slowly, in the board and among the directors and vice presidents, people subtly oppose the chief's methods and spirit. They quietly undermine his measures, obstruct his plans, thwart his policies. Where the chief once enjoyed cooperation and support, he meets inertia and indifference until at last he resigns from sheer inability to carry out policy.[1] In the same way, appointing leaders with a secular or materialistic outlook prevents the Holy Spirit from making spiritual progress in that place.

The Holy Spirit does not take control of anyone against his or her will. When people who lack spiritual fitness are elected to leadership positions, He quietly withdraws and leaves them to implement their own policies according to their own standards, but without His aid. The inevitable result is an unspiritual administration.

The church at Jerusalem listened to the apostles' instructions and selected seven men who possessed the one necessary qualification. As a result of their Spirit-filled work, the church was blessed: the men selected to distribute food and earthly care were soon seen as the Spirit's agents in dispensing heavenly blessings. Stephen became the first martyr for Christ, and his death played a large role in the conversion of Paul. Philip became an evangelist and was used by the Spirit to lead the great revival in Samaria. Leaders who are faithful in the exercise of their gifts prepare the way for promotion to greater responsibilities and usefulness.

The book of Acts clearly demonstrates that leaders who significantly influenced the Christian movement were Spirit-filled. It is reported of Him who commanded His disciples to tarry in Jerusalem until they were endued with power from on high that He Himself was "anointed . . . with the Holy Spirit and power" (10:38). Those 120 in the upper room were all filled with the Spirit (2:4). Peter was filled with the

Spirit when he addressed the Sanhedrin (4:8). Stephen, filled with the Spirit, bore witness to Christ and died a radiant martyr (6:3; 7:55). In the Spirit's fullness Paul began and completed his unique ministry (9:17; 13:9). Paul's missionary companion Barnabas was filled with the Spirit (11:24). We would be strangely blind not to see this obvious requirement for spiritual leadership.

These early leaders of the church were sensitive to the leading of the Spirit. Because they had surrendered their own wills to the Spirit's control, they were delighted to obey His promptings and guidance. Philip left the revival in Samaria to go to the desert, but what a convert he found there (8:29)! The Spirit helped Peter to overcome his bias and meet with Cornelius, which led to blessings for the Gentile world (10:19; 11:12). The Spirit called Paul and Barnabas as first missionaries of the church (13:1-4). Throughout his busy life, Paul obeyed the Spirit's restraints and constraints (16:6-7; 19:21; 20:22). The leaders of the church at Jerusalem submitted to the Spirit. "It seemed good to the Holy Spirit and to us" was how the council articulated their judgments (15:28).

The Spirit intervened to bring the gospel to the Gentiles. The Spirit's great purpose is missions. Should that not be ours too?

Just now as I write, the Spirit is moving among Asian churches, giving them a new missionary vision and passion. Japanese churches have sent missionaries from Taiwan to Brazil. While the number of North American and European missionaries remains static, the heavenly Strategist is awakening the Asian church to her missionary obligations. Recently, more than three thousand Third World Christians have obeyed the call of God to missions.

Paul counseled leaders in the church at Ephesus on how to understand their office. "Keep watch over yourselves and all the flock of which the Holy Spirit has made you overseers" (Acts 20:28). Those leaders did not hold office by apostolic selection or popular election but by divine appointment. They were accountable not only to the church but also to the Holy Spirit. What a sense of assurance and responsibility, what a spiritual authority this teaching brought them, and brings to us!

Without the filling of the Holy Spirit at Pentecost, how could the apostles have faced the superhuman task ahead? They needed supernatural power for their truceless warfare against the devil and hell (Luke 24:29; Ephesians 6:10–18).

To be filled with the Spirit means simply that the Christian voluntarily surrenders life and will to the Spirit. Through faith, the believer's personality is permeated, mastered, and controlled by the Spirit. The meaning of "filled" is not to "pour into a passive container" but to "take possession of the mind." That's the meaning found in Luke 5:26: "They were filled with awe." When we invite the Spirit to fill us, the Spirit's power grips our lives with this kind of strength and passion.

To be filled with the Spirit is to be controlled by the Spirit. The Christian leader's mind, emotions, will, and physical strength all become available for the Spirit to guide and use. Under the Spirit's control, natural gifts of leadership are lifted to their highest power, sanctified for holy purpose. Through the work of the now ungrieved and unhindered Spirit, all the fruits of the Spirit start to grow in the leader's life. His witness is more winsome, service more steady, and testimony more powerful. All real Christian service is but the expression of Spirit power through believers yielded to Him (John 7:37–39).

If we pretend to be filled, or hold back on our willingness to let the Spirit control us, we create the kind of trouble A. W. Tozer warns against:

> No one whose senses have been exercised to know good or evil can but grieve over the sight of zealous souls seeking to be filled with the Holy Spirit while they are living in a state of moral carelessness and borderline sin. Whoever would be indwelt by the Spirit must judge his life for any hidden iniquities. He must expel from his heart everything that is out of accord with the character of God as revealed by the Holy Scriptures. . . . There can be no tolerance of evil, no laughing off the things that God hates.[2]

The filling of the Spirit is essential for spiritual leadership. And each believer has as much of the Spirit's presence as he or she will ever need. Our task is to remain yielded to Him.

Spiritual Gifts

Christians everywhere have undiscovered and unused spiritual gifts. The leader must help bring those gifts into the service of the kingdom, to develop them, to marshal their power. Spirituality alone does not make a leader; natural gifts and those given by God must be there too.

In our warfare against evil, we need the supernatural equipment God has provided in the spiritual gifts given to the church. To be used effectively, those gifts must be enriched by spiritual grace.

Often, though not always, the Holy Spirit imparts gifts that naturally fit the character and personality of the Christian leader. And the Spirit raises those gifts to a new level of effectiveness. Samuel Chadwick, the noted Methodist preacher, said that when he was filled with the Spirit, he did not receive a new brain but a new mentality; not a new tongue but new speaking effectiveness; not a new language but a new Bible. Chadwick's natural qualities were given a new vitality, a new energy.

The coming of spiritual gifts in the life of the Christian does not eliminate natural gifts but enhances and stimulates them. New birth in Christ does not change natural qualities but brings them in line with holy purpose; when they are placed under the control of the Holy Spirit, they are raised to new effectiveness. Hidden abilities are often released.

The one called by God to spiritual leadership can be confident that the Holy Spirit has given him or her all necessary gifts for the service at hand.

FOR REFLECTION

    A. How do you understand from Scripture what it means to be "Spirit-filled"?

    B. How have you experienced being filled with the Holy Spirit?

    C. In what ways have your experiences in leadership been affected by the presence or absence of the Holy Spirit?

11
PRAYER AND
LEADERSHIP

*I urge then, first of all, that requests, prayers, intercession
and thanksgiving be made for everyone. . . .*

1 Timothy 2:1

The spiritual leader should outpace the rest of the church, above all, in prayer. And yet the most advanced leader is conscious of the possibility of endless development in his prayer life. Nor does he ever feel that he has "already attained." Dean C. J. Vaughan once said: "If I wished to humble anyone, I should question him about his prayers. I know nothing to compare with this topic for its sorrowful self-confessions."

Prayer is the most ancient, most universal, and most intensive expression of the religious instinct. It includes the simplest speech of infant lips, and the sublime entreaties of older age. All reach the Majesty on high. Prayer is indeed the Christian's vital breath and native air.

But, strange paradox, most of us find it hard to pray. We do not naturally delight in drawing near to God. We sometimes pay lip service to the delight and power of prayer. We call it indispensable; we know the Scriptures call for it. Yet we often fail to pray.

Let us take encouragement from the lives of saintly leaders who overcame this natural reluctance and became mighty in prayer. Of Samuel Chadwick it was said:

> He was essentially a man of prayer. Every morning he would be astir shortly after six o'clock, and he kept a little room which was his private sanctum for his quiet hour before breakfast. He was mighty in public prayer because he was constant in private devotion. . . . When he prayed he expected God to do something. "I wish I had prayed more," he wrote toward the end of his life, "even if I had worked less; and from the bottom of my heart I wish I had prayed better."[1]

"When I go to prayer," confessed an eminent Christian, "I find my heart so loath to go to God, and when it is with Him, so loath to stay." Then he pointed to the need for self-discipline. "When you feel most indisposed to pray, yield not to it," he counseled, "but strive and endeavor to pray, even when you think you cannot."

Mastering the art of prayer, like anything else, takes time. The time we give it will be a true measure of its importance to us. We always find the time for important things. The most common excuse for little time spent in prayer is the list of "to-dos" that crowd our day—all our many duties. To Martin Luther, an extra load of duties was reason enough to pray more, not less. Hear his plans for the next day's work: "Work, work from early till late. In fact I have so much to do that I shall spend the first three hours in prayer."

If Luther was busy, and prayed, so can we.

Try to explain exactly how prayer works and you will quickly run against some very difficult puzzles. But people who are skeptical of prayer's validity and power are usually those who do not practice it seriously or fail to obey when God reveals His will. We cannot learn about prayer except by praying. No philosophy has ever taught a soul to pray. The intellectual problems associated with prayer are met in the joy of answered prayer and closer fellowship with God.

The Christian leader who seeks an example to follow does well to turn to the life of Jesus Himself. Our belief in the necessity of prayer comes from observing His life. Surely if anyone could have sustained life without prayer, it would be the very Son of God Himself. If prayer is silly or unnecessary, Jesus would not have wasted His time at it. But wait! Prayer was the dominant feature of His life and a recurring part of His teaching. Prayer kept His moral vision sharp and clear. Prayer gave Him courage to endure the perfect but painful will of His Father. Prayer paved the way for transfiguration. To Jesus, prayer was not a hasty add-on, but a joyous necessity.

> *In Luke 5:16 we have a general statement which throws a vivid light on the daily practice of the Lord. "And He withdrew Himself in the deserts and prayed." It is not of one occasion but of many that the evangelist speaks in this place. It was our Lord's habit to seek retirement for prayer. When He withdrew Himself from men, He was accustomed to press far into the uninhabited country—He was in the deserts. The surprise of the onlookers lay in this, that one so mighty, so richly endowed with spiritual power, should find it necessary for Himself to repair to the source of strength, that there He might refresh His weary spirit. To us, the wonder is still greater, that He, the prince of Life, the Eternal word, the Only-begotten of the Father, should prostrate Himself in meekness before the throne of God, making entreaty for grace to help in time of need.[2]*

Christ spent full nights in prayer (Luke 6:12). He often rose before dawn to have unbroken communion with His Father (Mark 1:35). The great crises of His life and ministry began with periods of special prayer, as in Luke 5:16: "Jesus often withdrew to lonely places and prayed"—a statement that indicates a regular habit. By word and example He instructed His disciples on the importance of solitude in prayer (Mark 6:46, following the feeding of the five thousand; Luke 9:28, preceding the Transfiguration). To the person on whom devolves the responsibility for selecting personnel for specific spiritual responsibilities, the example of the Lord's spending the night in prayer before making His choice of apostles (Luke 6:12) is luminous.

Both our Lord and His bond slave Paul made clear that true prayer is not dreamy reverie. "All vital praying makes a drain on a man's vitality. True intercession is a sacrifice, a bleeding sacrifice," wrote J. H. Jowett. Jesus performed miracles without a sign of outward strain, but "he offered up prayers and petitions with loud cries and tears" (Hebrews 5:7).

Sometimes our prayers are pale and weak compared to those of Paul or Epaphras. "Epaphras . . . is always wrestling in prayer for you," wrote Paul in Colossians 4:12. And to the same group: "I want you to know how much I am struggling for you" (Colossians 2:1). The Greek word used for "struggle" here is the root for our words "agony" and "agonize." It is used to describe a person struggling at work until utterly weary (Colossians 1:29) or competing in the arena for an athletic prize (1 Corinthians 9:25). It describes a soldier battling for his life (1 Timothy 6:12), or a man struggling to deliver his friends from danger (John 18:36). True prayer is a strenuous spiritual exercise that demands the utmost mental discipline and concentration.

We are encouraged to note that Paul, probably the greatest human champion of prayer, confessed, "We do not know what we ought to pray for." And then he hastened to add, "The Spirit intercedes for us with groans that words cannot express. And he who searches our hearts knows the mind of the Spirit, because the Spirit intercedes for the saints in accordance with God's will" (Romans 8:26–28). The Spirit joins us in prayer and pours His supplications into our own.

Pray in the Spirit

All Christians need more teaching in the art of prayer, and the Holy Spirit is the master teacher. The Spirit's help in prayer is mentioned in the Bible more frequently than any other help He gives us. All true praying comes from the Spirit's activity in our souls. Both Paul and Jude teach that effective prayer is "praying in the Spirit." That phrase means that we pray along the same lines, about the same things, in the same name, as the Holy Spirit. True prayer rises in the spirit of the Christian from the Spirit who indwells us.

To pray in the Spirit is important for two reasons. First, we are to pray in the realm of the Spirit, for the Holy Spirit is the sphere and atmosphere of the Christian's life. In this we often fail. Much praying is physical rather than spiritual, in the realm of the mind alone, the product of our own thinking and not of the Spirit's teaching. But real prayer is deeper. It uses the body, requires the cooperation of the mind, and moves in the supernatural realm of the Spirit. Such praying transacts its business in the heavenly realm.

Second, we are to pray in the power and energy of the Spirit. "Give yourselves wholly to prayer and entreaty; pray on every occasion in the power of the Spirit" (Ephesians 6:18 NEB). For its superhuman task, prayer demands more than human power. We have the Spirit of power as well as the Spirit of prayer. All the human energy of heart, mind, and will can achieve great human results, but praying in the Holy Spirit releases supernatural resources.

The Spirit delights to help us pray. In each of our three chief handicaps, we can count on the Spirit's help. Sometimes we are kept from prayer by sin in our heart. As we grow in trust and submission, the Holy Spirit leads us to the blood of Christ, which cleanses every stain.

Sometimes the ignorance of our minds hinders our prayers. But the Spirit knows the mind of God and shares that knowledge with us as we wait and listen. The Spirit does this by giving us a clear conviction that a particular prayer request is part of God's will for us, or not.

Sometimes we are earthbound because of the infirmity of the body. We get sick, we feel ill, we are weak. The Spirit will quicken our bodies and enable us to rise above weaknesses, even those imposed by sultry tropical climates.

Then, as if these three conditions were not enough, the spiritual leader must oppose Satan in prayer. Satan will try to depress, to create doubt and discouragement, to keep a leader from communion with God. In the Holy Spirit, we have a heavenly ally against this supernatural foe.

Spiritual leaders should know the experience of praying in the Spirit as part of their daily walk. Do we ever try to live independently of the Spirit? Do we fail to see full answers to prayer? We can read all day about prayer, and experience little of its power, and so stunt our service.

The Bible often explains prayer as spiritual warfare. "For our struggle is . . . against the rulers, against the authorities, against the powers of this dark world and against the spiritual forces of evil in the heavenly realms" (Ephesians 6:12). In this struggle phase of prayer, three personalities are engaged. Between God and the devil stands the Christian at prayer. Though weak alone, the Christian plays a strategic role in the struggle between the dragon and the Lamb. The praying Christian wields no personal power, but power nonetheless delegated by the victorious Christ to whom that faithful believer is united by faith. Faith is like a reticulating system through which the victory won on Calvary reaches the devil's captives and delivers them from darkness into light.

Jesus was not so much concerned over wicked people and their deeds as with the forces of evil that caused those people to sin. Behind Peter's denial and Judas's betrayal was the sinister hand of Satan. "Get thee behind me, Satan," was the Lord's response to Peter's presumptuous rebuke. All around us are people bound in sin, captives to the devil. Our prayers should ascend not only for them but against Satan who holds them as his prize. Satan must be compelled to relax his grip, and this can only be achieved by Christ's victory on the cross.

As Jesus dealt with sin's cause rather than effect, so the spiritual leader should adopt the same method in prayer. And the leader must know how to help those under his charge who are also involved in that same spiritual warfare.

In a telling illustration, Jesus compared Satan to a strong man, fully armed. Before anyone can enter such a man's house and set captives free, the man must first be bound. Only then can a rescue succeed (Matthew 12:29). What could it mean to "tie up the strong man" except to neutralize his might through the overcoming power of Christ who came "to destroy (nullify, render inoperative) the works of the devil"? And how can that happen except by the prayer of faith that lays hold of the victory of Calvary and claims it for the problem at hand? We cannot hope to effect a rescue from Satan's den without first disarming the adversary. God makes available His divine authority through prayer, and we can confidently claim it. Jesus promised His disciples: "I have given you authority . . . to overcome all the power of the enemy" (Luke 10:19).

The spiritual leader will be alert to the most effective way to influence people. Hudson Taylor is well known for his expression, "It is possible to move men, through God, by prayer alone." During his missionary career he demonstrated the truth of his claim a thousand times.

Practice

It is one thing to believe such power is available in prayer, but another thing to practice it. People are difficult to move; it is much easier to pray for things or provisions than to deal with the stubbornness of the human heart. But in just these intricate situations, the leader must use God's power to move human hearts in the direction he believes to be the will of God. Through prayer the leader has the key to that complicated lock.

It is the supreme dignity and glory of the human creature to be able to say yes or no to God. Humans have been given free will. But this poses a problem. If by prayer we can influence the conduct of others, does such power encroach on free will? Will God temper one person's freedom to answer another person's prayer? It seems difficult to imagine. And yet, if prayers cannot influence the course of events, why pray?

The first point to make is that God is consistent with Himself always. God does not contradict Himself. When God promises to answer prayer, the answer will come—always in a manner consistent with divine nature, for "he cannot disown himself" (2 Timothy 2:13). No word or action from God will contradict any other word or action of God.

The second point in resolving these questions is that prayer is a divine ordinance. God has commanded prayer, and we can be confident that as we meet revealed conditions for prayer, answers will be granted. God sees no contradiction between human free will and divine response to prayer. When God commands us to pray "for kings and those in authority," there is implied power to influence the course of men and events. If not, why pray? Our obligation to pray stands above any dilemma concerning the effects of prayer.

Third, we can know the will of God concerning the prayer we raise.

Our capacity to know God's will is the basis for all prayers of faith. God can speak to us clearly through our mind and heart. The Bible instructs us directly concerning the will of God on all matters of principle. In our hearts the Holy Spirit ministers to instruct us in the will of God (Romans 8:26–27). As we patiently seek the will of God concerning our petition, the Spirit will impress our minds and convince our hearts. Such God-given conviction leads us beyond the prayer of hope to the prayer of faith.

When God lays a burden on our hearts and thus keeps us praying, He obviously intends to grant the answer. George Mueller was asked if he really believed that two men would be converted, men for whom Mueller had prayed for over fifty years. Mueller replied: "Do you think God would have kept me praying all these years if He did not intend to save them?" In fact, both men were converted, one shortly after Mueller's death.[3]

In prayer we deal directly with God and only in a secondary sense other people. The goal of prayer is the ear of God. Prayer moves others through God's influence on them. It is not our prayer that moves people, but the God to whom we pray.

> *Prayer moves the arm*
> *That moves the world*
> *To bring deliverance down.*
> **Author unknown**

To move people, the leader must be able to move God, for God has made it clear that He moves people in response to prayer. If a scheming Jacob was given "power with God and with men," then surely any leader who follows God's prayer principles can enjoy the same power (Genesis 32:28).

Prevailing prayer that moves people is the outcome of a right relationship with God. The Bible is very clear on the reasons why prayers go unanswered, and every reason centers on the believer's relationship with God. God will not cooperate with prayers of mere self-interest, or prayers that come from impure motives. The Christian who clings to sin closes the ear of God. Least of all will God tolerate unbelief, the chief of sins. "Anyone who comes to him must believe" (Hebrews 11:6). In all our prayers the paramount motive is the glory of God.

Great leaders of the Bible were great at prayer. "They were not leaders because of brilliancy of thought, because they were exhaustless in resources, because of their magnificent culture or native endowment, but because, by the power of prayer, they could command the power of God."[4]

FOR REFLECTION

A. The school of prayer begins with a kindergarten understanding of communion with God and proceeds beyond graduate studies—in what grade is your prayer life? What progress have you made recently?

B. Who are your prayer models? How well do you understand the way they practice prayer?

C. What helpful thoughts or insights on prayer will you remember from this chapter?

12
THE LEADER
AND TIME

Make the best use of your time. . . .

Ephesians 5:16 Phillips

The quality of a person's leadership will be in part measured by time: its use and its passage. The character and career of a young person depends on how he or she spends spare time. We cannot regulate school or office hours—those are determined for us—but we can say what we will do before and after those commitments. The way we employ the surplus hours, after provision has been made for work, meals, and sleep, will determine if we develop into mediocre or powerful people. Leisure is a glorious opportunity and a subtle danger. A discretionary hour can be wisely invested or foolishly wasted. Each moment of the day is a gift from God that deserves care, for by any measure, our time is short and the work is great.

Minutes and hours wisely used translate into an abundant life. On one occasion when Michelangelo was pressing himself to finish a work on deadline, someone warned him, "This may cost your life!" He replied, "What else is life for?"

Hours and days will surely pass, but we can direct them purposefully and productively. Philosopher William James affirmed that the best use of one's life is to spend it for something that will outlast it. Life's value is not its duration but its donation—not how long we live but how fully and how well.[1]

Time is precious, but we squander it thoughtlessly. Moses knew time was valuable and prayed to be taught to measure it by days, not by years (Psalm 90:12). If we are careful about days, the years will take care of themselves.

A leader will seldom say, "I don't have the time." Such an excuse is usually the refuge of a small-minded and inefficient person. Each of us has the time to do the whole will of God for our lives. J. H. Jowett said:

> I think one of the cant phrases of our day is the familiar one
> by which we express our permanent want of time. We repeat it
> so often that by the very repetition we have deceived ourselves
> into believing it. It is never the supremely busy men who have
> no time. So compact and systematic is the regulation of their
> day that whenever you make a demand on them, they seem to
> find additional corners to offer for unselfish service. I confess
> as a minister, that the men to whom I most hopefully look for
> additional service are the busiest men.

Our problem is not too little time but making better use of the time we have. Each of us has as much time as anyone else. The president of the United States has the same twenty-four hours as we. Others may surpass our abilities, influence, or money, but no one has more time.

As in the parable of the pounds (minas in the NIV; Luke 19:12–27), where each servant was given the same amount of money, we each have been given the same amount of time. But few of us use it so wisely as to produce a tenfold return. The parable recognizes different abilities; the servant with less capacity but equal faithfulness received the same reward. We are not responsible for our endowments or natural abilities, but we are responsible for the strategic use of time.

When Paul urged the Ephesians to "redeem" the time (see 5:16 KJV), he was treating time like purchasing power. We exchange time in the market of life for certain occupations and activities that may be worthy or not, productive or not. Another translation renders the verse "Buy up the opportunities," for time is opportunity. Herein lies the importance of a carefully planned life: "If we progress in the economy of time, we are learning to live. If we fail here, we fail everywhere."

Time lost can never be retrieved. Time cannot be hoarded, only spent well. These lines were found engraved on a sundial:

> *The shadow of my finger cast*
> *Divides the future from the past;*
> *Before it stands the unborn hour*
> *In darkness and beyond thy power;*
> *Behind its unreturning line*
> *The vanished hour, no longer thine;*
> *One hour alone is in thy hands,*
> *The* now *on which the shadow stands.*
> **Author Unknown**

In the face of this sobering reality, the leader must carefully select priorities. He or she must thoughtfully weigh the value of different opportunities and responsibilities. The leader cannot spend time on secondary matters while essential obligations scream for attention. A day needs careful planning. The person who wants to excel must select and reject, then concentrate on the most important items.

It is often helpful to keep records of how each hour in a given week is spent, and then look at the record in the light of scriptural priorities. The results may be shocking. Often the record shows that we have much more time available for Christian service than we imagine.

Suppose that we allot ourselves a generous eight hours a day for sleep (and few need more than that), three hours for meals and conversation, ten hours for work and travel. Still we have thirty-five hours each week to fill. What happens to them? How are they invested? A person's entire contribution to the kingdom of God may turn on how those hours are used. Certainly those hours determine whether life is commonplace or extraordinary.

The intrepid missionary Mary Slessor was the daughter of a drunkard. At age eleven she began working in a factory in Dundee, and there spent her days from six in the morning until six at night. Yet that grueling regimen did not prevent her from educating herself for a notable career.[2]

David Livingstone, at age ten, worked in a cotton mill in Dumbarton fourteen hours a day. Surely he had excuses for not studying, for not redeeming the little leisure left to him. But he learned Latin and could read Horace and Virgil at age sixteen. At age twenty-seven, he had finished a program in both medicine and theology.

Similar examples are so numerous that we have little ground today to plead insufficient time for achieving something worthwhile in life.

Our Lord sets the perfect example of strategic use of time. He moved through life with measured steps, never hurried, though always surrounded by demands and crowds. When a person approached Him for help, Jesus gave the impression that He had no more important concern than the needs of His visitor.

The secret of Jesus' serenity lay in His assurance that He was working according to the Father's plan for His life—a plan that embraced every hour and made provision for every need. Through communion in prayer with His Father, Jesus received each day both the words He would say and the works He would do. "The words I say to you are not just my own. Rather, it is the Father, living in me, who is doing his work" (John 14:10).

Jesus' greatest concern was to fulfill the work committed to Him within the allotted hours. He was conscious of a divine timing in His life (John 7:6; 12:23,27; 13:1; 17:1). Even to His beloved mother He said, "My time has not yet come" (John 2:4). Responding to Mary and Martha's distress, Jesus declined to change His schedule by two days (John 11:1–6). When He reviewed His life at its close, He said: "I have brought you glory on earth by completing the work you gave me to do" (John 17:4). Jesus completed His life's work without any part spoiled by undue haste or half done through lack of time. His twenty-four hours a day was sufficient to complete the whole will of God.

Jesus told His disciples: "Are there not twelve hours in the day?"

J. Stuart Holden saw in our Lord's words both the shortness of time and the sufficiency of time. There were indeed twelve hours in the day, but in fact there were fully twelve hours in the day.[3]

Conscious of time, Jesus spent His time doing things that mattered. No time was wasted on things not vital. The strength of moral character is conserved by refusing the unimportant.

> *No trifling in this life of mine;*
> *Not this the path the blessed Master trod;*
> *But every hour and power employed*
> *Always and all for God.*
>
> **Author unknown**

How interesting that the Gospel accounts contain no hint of any interruption ever disturbing the serenity of the Son of God. Few things are more likely to produce tension in a busy life than unexpected interruptions. Yet to Jesus there were no such things. "Unexpected" events were always foreseen in the Father's planning, and Jesus was therefore undisturbed by them. True, at times there was hardly time to eat, but time was always sufficient to accomplish all the Father's will.

Often the pressure a spiritual leader feels comes from assuming tasks that God has not assigned; for such tasks the leader cannot expect God to supply the extra strength required.

One busy man told me how he mastered the problem of interruptions. "Up to some years ago," he testified, "I was always annoyed by them, which was really a form of selfishness on my part. People used to walk in and say, 'Well, I just had two hours to kill here in between trains, and I thought I would come and see you.' That used to bother me. Then the Lord convinced me that He sends people our way. He sent Philip to the Ethiopian eunuch. He sent Barnabas to see Saul. The same applies today. God sends people our way.

"So when someone comes in, I say, 'The Lord must have brought you here. Let us find out why He sent you. Let us have prayer.' Well this does two things. The interview takes on new importance because God is in it. And it generally shortens the interview. If a visitor knows you are looking for reasons why God should have brought him, and there are none apparent, the visit becomes pleasant but brief.

"So now I take interruptions as from the Lord. They belong in my schedule, because the schedule is God's to arrange at His pleasure."

Paul affirms that God has a plan for every life. We have been created "in Christ Jesus to do good works, which God prepared in advance for us to do" (Ephesians 2:10). Through daily prayer, the leader discovers the details of that plan and arranges work accordingly. Each half hour should carry its load of usefulness.

John Wesley and F. B. Meyer, men who influenced the world for Christ, divided their days into five-minute periods, then tried to make each one count. All of us could benefit by similar discipline. For example, much reading can be done during otherwise wasted minutes.

Meyer's biographer tells how he would redeem the time:

> If he had a long railway journey before him, he would settle himself in his corner of the railway carriage, open his dispatch case which was fitted as a sort of stationery cabinet, and set to work on some abstruse article, quite oblivious of his surroundings. Often at protracted conventions, and even in committee meetings, when the proceeding did not demand his undivided attention, he would unobtrusively open his case and proceed to answer letters.[4]

Another miser with time was W. E. Sangster. His son writes of him:

> Time was never wasted. The difference between one minute and two was of considerable consequence to him. He would appear from his study. "My boy, you're not doing anything. I have exactly twenty-two minutes. We'll go for a walk. We can walk right around the common in that time." He then hurtled out of the house at tremendous speed and I normally had to run to catch up. He would then discourse on current affairs (five minutes), Surrey's prospects in the country championship (two minutes), the necessity for revival (five minutes), the reality of the Loch Ness monster (two minutes), and the

sanctity of William Romaine (three minutes). By that time we would be home again.[5]

A leader needs a balanced approach to time lest it become his bondage and downfall. Without a grip on time, the leader works under unnecessary strain. Even when the leader has done the utmost to fulfill daily obligations, vast areas of work always remain. Every call for help is not necessarily a call from God, for it is impossible to respond to every need. If the leader sincerely plans his day in prayer, then executes the plan with all energy and eagerness, that is enough. A leader is responsible only for what lies within the range of control. The rest he should trust to our loving and competent heavenly Father.

Procrastination, the thief of time, is one of the devil's most potent weapons for defrauding us of eternal heritage. The habit of "putting off" is fatal to spiritual leadership. Its power resides in our natural reluctance to come to grips with important decisions. Making decisions, and acting on them, always requires moral energy. But the passing of time never makes action easier, quite the opposite. Most decisions are more difficult a day later, and you may also lose an advantage by such delay. The nettle will never be easier to grasp than now.

"Do it now" is a motto that has led many people to worldly success, and it is equally relevant in spiritual matters. A helpful method for overcoming procrastination is to carefully set deadlines, and never miss or postpone even one.

A lifelong reader was asked by friends, "How do you get time for it?" He replied, "I don't get time for it; I take time."[6]

FOR REFLECTION

A. What three areas of your life do you think would be improved as a result of better use of time?

B. What does "redeeming time" (Ephesians 5:16) mean to you?

C. How do you deal with tendencies to procrastinate?

13

THE LEADER
AND READING

When you come, bring . . . my scrolls, especially the parchments.

2 Timothy 4:13

Reading maketh a full man; speaking, a ready man, writing, an exact man.

Bacon

Paul's counsel to Timothy, "Give heed to reading" (see 1 Timothy 4:13), surely referred to the public reading of the Old Testament. But Paul's advice is appropriate for other areas of reading as well. Paul's books—the ones he wanted Timothy to bring along—were probably works of Jewish history, explanations of the law and prophets, and perhaps some of the heathen poets Paul quoted in his sermons and lectures. A student to the end, Paul wanted to spend time in study.

During his imprisonment and shortly before his martyrdom in 1536, William Tyndale wrote to the governor-in-chief, asking that some goods be sent him:

> *A warmer cap, a candle, a piece of cloth to patch my leggings.
> . . . But above all, I beseech and entreat your clemency to
> be urgent with the Procureur that he may kindly permit me
> to have my Hebrew Bible, Hebrew grammar and Hebrew
> Dictionary, that I many spend time with that in study.*[1]

Both Paul and Tyndale devoted last days on earth to the study of the parchments. Spiritual leaders of every generation will have a consuming passion to know the Word of God through diligent study and the illumination of the Holy Spirit. But in this chapter our special interest is a leader's supplementary reading.

The leader who intends to grow spiritually and intellectually will be reading constantly. Lawyers must read steadily to keep up on case law. Doctors must read to stay current in the ever-changing world of health care. So the spiritual leader must master God's Word and its principles, and know as well the minds of those who look to the leader for guidance. To do so, the leader must have an active life of reading.

These days, the practice of reading spiritual classics is on the wane. We have more leisure today than ever before in history, but many people claim to have no time for reading. A spiritual leader cannot use that excuse.

John Wesley had a passion for reading, and he did so mostly on horseback. Often he rode a horse fifty and sometimes ninety miles in a day. His habit was to ride with a volume of science or history or medicine propped in the pommel of his saddle, and thus he consumed thousands of books. Besides his Greek New Testament, three great books took possession of Wesley's mind and heart during his Oxford days: *Imitation of Christ, Holy Living and Dying,* and *The Serious Call.* These three were his spiritual guides. Wesley told the younger ministers of the Methodist societies to read or get out of the ministry!

Leaders should determine to spend a minimum of half an hour a day reading books that feed the soul and stimulate the mind. In a perceptive series on "The Use and Abuse of Books," A. W. Tozer said:

> *Why does today's Christian find the reading of great books always beyond him? Certainly intellectual powers do not wane from one generation to another. We are as smart as our father, and any thought they could entertain we can entertain if we are sufficiently interested to make the effort. The major cause of the decline in the quality of current Christian literature is*

*not intellectual but spiritual. To enjoy a great religious book
requires a degree of consecration to God and detachment from
the world that few modern Christians have. The early Christian
Fathers, the Mystics, the Puritans, are not hard to understand,
but they inhabit the highlands where the air is crisp and
rarefied, and none but the God-enamored can come. . . . One
reason why people are unable to understand great Christian
classics is that they are trying to understand without any
intention of obeying them.*[2]

Why Read?

"Read to refill the wells of inspiration," was the advice of Harold
Ockenga, who took a suitcase of books on his honeymoon![3]

Bacon's famous rule for reading: "Read not to contradict or confute,
nor to believe and take for granted, nor to find talk and discourse, but
to weigh and consider. Some books are to be tested, others to be swal-
lowed, and some few to be chewed and digested."[4] Indeed, if we read
merely to stock our head with ideas, to feel superior to others, or to
appear learned, then our reading is useless and vain.

The spiritual leader should choose books for their spiritual benefit.
Some authors challenge heart and conscience and point us toward the
highest; they spark our impulse to service and lead us to God.

Spiritual leaders should also read for intellectual growth. This will
require books that test wits, provide fresh ideas, challenge assump-
tions, and probe complexities.

The leader should read to cultivate his preaching and writing style.
For that, we need to read those masters who instruct us in the art of
incisive and compelling speech. Tozer recommended John Bunyan
for simplicity, Joseph Addison for clarity and elegance, John Milton
for nobility and consistent elevation of thought, Charles Dickens for
sprightliness, and Francis Bacon for dignity.

The leader should read, too, to acquire new information, to keep
current with the time, to be well informed in his or her own field of
expertise.

The leader should read to have fellowship with great minds. Through books we hold communion with the greatest spiritual leaders of the ages.

A good book has great power. In *Curiosities of Literature*, Benjamin Disraeli gives a number of instances where a person has been magnificently influenced by a solitary book. As I have read the biographies of great Christians, time and again one book has brought their lives to crisis and produced a revolution of ministry. That book is Charles G. Finney's *Lectures on Revivals of Religion*.[5]

What to Read

If a man is known by the company he keeps, so also his character is reflected in the books he reads. A leader's reading is the outward expression of his inner aspirations. The vast number of titles pouring from presses today makes discriminating choice essential. We can afford to read only the best, only that which invigorates our mission. Our reading should be regulated by who we are and what we intend to accomplish.

An old author whose pen name was Cladius Clear said that a reader could divide his books as he would people. A few were "lovers," and those books would go with him into exile. Others are "friends." Most books are "acquaintances," works with which he was on nodding terms.

Matthew Arnold thought that the best of literature was bound within five hundred book covers. Daniel Webster preferred to master a few books rather than read widely. To them he would appeal for genuine knowledge of the human heart, its aspirations and tragedies, hopes and disappointments. Indiscriminate reading serves no one well. Hobbes, the English philosopher, once said, "If I had read as many books as other people, I would know as little."

Samuel Brengle said this about poetry:

> I like the poets whose writings reveal great moral character and passion—such as Tennyson and some of Browning. The works of others have light, but I prefer flame to light. Shakespeare?

A mind as clear as a sunbeam—but passionless, light without heat. Shelley? Keats? There's a sense in which they were perfect poets, but they don't move me. Beautiful—but wordmongers. There's an infinite difference between the beauty of holiness and the holiness of beauty. One leads to the highest, loftiest, most Godlike character; the other often—too often—leads to an orgy of sensation.[6]

Sir W. Robertson Nicoll, for many years editor of *British Weekly*, found biography the most attractive form of general reading because biography transmits personality. To read the lives of great and consecrated men and women is to kindle one's own heart toward God. Imagine how the missions movement has been inspired by the biographies of William Carey, Adoniram Judson, Hudson Taylor, Charles Studd, or Albert Simpson.[7]

Joseph W. Kemp, widely known for his preaching and teaching, always kept a good biography on hand. Ransome W. Cooper wrote:

The reading of good biography forms an important part of a Christian's education. It provides him with numberless illustrations for use in his own service. He learns to assess the true worth of character, to glimpse a work goal for his own life, to decide how best to attain it, what self-denial is needed to curb unworthy aspirations; and all the time he learns how God breaks into the dedicated life to bring about his own purposes.

A leader should neither be content with easy books nor satisfied with reading only in his specialty. Muriel Ormrod counseled:

It is better that we should always tackle something a bit beyond us. We should always aim to read something different—not only the writers with whom we agree, but those with whom we are ready to do battle. And let us not condemn them out of hand because they do not agree with us; their point of view challenges us to examine the truth and to test their views against Scripture. And let us not comment on nor criticize writers of whom we have heard only second-hand, or third-hand, without troubling to read their works for ourselves. . . . Don't be afraid of new ideas—and don't be carried away with them either.[8]

The leader should immerse himself in books that equip him for higher service and leadership in the kingdom of God.

> *A little learning is a dangerous thing;*
> *Drink deep, or taste not the Pierian Spring;*
> *There shallow draughts intoxicate the brain,*
> *And drinking largely sobers us again.*
>
> **Alexander Pope**

How to Read

By reading we learn. By meditating on the themes of our reading, we pluck the fruit from the tree of books and add nourishment to our minds and our ministries. Unless our reading includes serious thinking, it is wasted time.

When Robert Southey, the poet, was telling a Quaker lady how he learned Portuguese grammar while he washed, and French literature while he dressed, and science while he took breakfast, and so on, filling his day utterly, she said quietly, "And when does thee think?" We can read without thinking, but such reading has not profit for us. Spurgeon counseled his students:

> *Master those books you have. Read them thoroughly. Bathe in them until they saturate you. Read and reread them, masticate and digest them. Let them go into your very self. Peruse a good book several times and make notes and analyses of it. A student will find that his mental constitution is more affected by one book thoroughly mastered than by twenty books he has merely skimmed. Little learning and much pride comes of hasty reading. Some men are disabled from thinking by their putting meditation away for the sake of much reading. In reading let your motto be "much, not many."*[9]

Use the following proven strategies for making your reading worth-while and profitable:

- What you intend to quickly forget, spend little time reading. The habit of reading and forgetting only builds the habit of forgetting other important matters.
- Use the same discrimination in choosing books as in choosing friends.
- Read with pencil and notebook in hand. Unless your memory is unusually retentive, much gained from reading is lost in a day. Develop a system of note taking. It will greatly help the memory.
- Have a "commonplace book," as they are called—a book to record what is striking, interesting, and worthy of second thought. In that way you will build a treasure trove of material for future use.
- Verify historical, scientific, and other data.
- Pass no word until its meaning is known. Keep a dictionary at hand.
- Vary your reading to keep your mind out of a rut. Variety is as refreshing to the mind as it is to the body.
- Correlate your reading—history with poetry, biography with historical novel. For example, when reading the history of the American Civil War, take up also the biography of Lincoln or Grant and the poetry of Whitman.

Canon Yates advised that every good book needs three readings. The first should be rapid and continuous, to give your mind an overview and to associate the book's material with your previous knowledge. The second reading should be careful and paced. Take notes and think. Then after an interval of time, a third reading should be like the first. Write a brief analysis of the book on the inside back cover. Thus will the book make a solid imprint on your memory.

A Scottish minister in Lumsden town had collected seventeen thousand volumes that he browsed with great delight. But his son said later, "Though he spent much time and pains on his sermons, he did not cut a channel between them and his reading."[10]

Beware the danger of the Lumsden syndrome. A book is a channel for the flow of ideas between one mind and another. The Lumsden preacher may have had the benefit of books for his own spiritual life, but the people in his church apparently never felt the influence of his reading. Leaders should always cut a channel between reading and speaking and writing, so that others derive benefit, pleasure, and inspiration.

A country minister in Australia known to this writer was a great book lover. Early in his ministry he determined to develop a biblically and theologically literate congregation. He helped his people learn to love books and led them into progressively deeper and weightier spiritual literature. The result is that a number of farmers in that district have significant libraries and thoughtful faith.

More ministers should try to lead in this way, guiding the church toward intelligent reading and larger, more committed, more resilient faith.

FOR REFLECTION

A. What books have had the greatest impact on your life? Why?

B. What book(s) would you be willing to read by the system advocated by Canon Yates (page 107)?

C. How many of the reading strategies listed on page 107 are you presently practicing when you read? Which ones do you think would be worth adding to your reading habits?

14
IMPROVING
LEADERSHIP

If you are a leader, exert yourself to lead.

Romans 12:8 NEB

Every Christian is obliged to be the best for God. Like any other worthwhile activity, if leadership can be improved, we should seek to improve it. In so doing, we prepare ourselves for higher service that may be just around the next corner, though unseen at the present.

Not every Christian is called to major leadership in the church, but every Christian is a leader, for we all influence others. All of us should strive to improve our leadership skills.

The first steps toward improvement involve recognizing weaknesses, making corrections, and cultivating strengths. Many reasons explain why church leadership is less than the best, and some of the following considerations may apply to you.

- Perhaps we lack a clearly defined goal that will stretch us, challenge faith, and unify life's activities.
- Perhaps our faith is timid, and we hesitate to take risks for the kingdom.

- Do we show the zeal of salvation in Christ, or is our demeanor morbid and sad? Enthusiastic leaders generate enthusiastic followers.
- We may be reluctant to grasp the nettle of a difficult situation and deal courageously with it. Or we may procrastinate, hoping that problems will vanish with time. The mediocre leader postpones difficult decisions, conversation, and letters. Delay solves nothing, and usually makes problems worse.
- Perhaps we sacrifice depth for breadth, and spreading ourselves thin, achieve only superficial results.

Exert Yourself to Lead

Romans 12:1 issues this imperative to leaders: "Offer your bodies as living sacrifices, holy and pleasing to God." The Greek aorist tense of the verb "offer" (which signifies a onetime act that is finished and done) is followed by thirty-six present-tense verbs (continuous action) that specify what should happen once we obey and offer. Two of those results are especially noteworthy here.

First, "exert yourself to lead" (Romans 12:8 NEB). Barclay translates this phrase, "If called upon to supply leadership, do it with zeal." Here is the summons to dive wholeheartedly into leadership, to serve with energy, to leave no room for sloth. Are we doing it?

Does your leadership show the intensity typical of Jesus? When the disciples saw the Master ablaze with righteous anger at the desecration of His Father's temple, they remembered the writings: "Zeal for your house will consume me" (John 2:17). So strong was Jesus' zeal that His friends thought He had abandoned common sense (Mark 3:21) and enemies charged Him with having a demon (John 7:20). Do people ever use "zeal" and your name in the same sentence?

Similar intensity marked Paul at every stage of his life. Wrote Adolph Deissman: "The lightning of the Damascus road found plenty of flammable material in the soul of the young persecutor. We see the flames shoot up, and we feel the glow then kindled lost none of its brightness in Paul the aged." We should strive for such continuing intensity as we grow older. Age tends to turn a flame into embers—the fire needs fresh fuel always.

Before his conversion, Paul's zeal drove him to terrible cruelty against the early Christians, such that he mourned over it later. That same zeal, cleansed and redirected by the Holy Spirit, carried into his new life in Christ and led to amazing achievements for the very church he once tried to destroy.

Full of the Spirit, Paul's mind was aflame with the truth of God and his heart glowed with God's love. At the center of his life was passion for the glory of God. No wonder people followed Paul. He exerted himself to lead. He did it with intensity and zeal. And the spirit of his life was contagious to those around him.

Kept at Boiling Point

Our second present-tense verb in Romans 12 comes from verse 11: "Never be lacking in zeal, but keep your spiritual fervor, serving the Lord." Harrington Lees translates this verse: "Not slothful in business, kept at boiling point by the Holy Spirit, doing bondservice for the master."

This verse points to the dynamic behind consistent, zealous service: "Kept at boiling point by the Holy Spirit." For most people in leadership, boiling points come easily on special occasions. Most leaders know times of great spiritual excitement, of the burning heart, of special nearness to God, and more than ordinary fruitfulness in service, but the problem is staying there! Verse 11 holds out the alluring possibility of living "aglow with the Spirit." We need not go off boil if the Spirit is the great central furnace of our lives.

Bunyan's Christian discovered this secret while visiting the Interpreter's house. He could not understand how the flames kept leaping higher while someone poured water on them. Then he saw another toward the rear pouring on the oil.[1]

In His great sermon on prayer, Jesus promised that the Holy Spirit would be given if only we ask. "If you then, though you are evil, know how to give good gifts to your children, how much more will your Father in heaven give the Holy Spirit to those who ask him!" (Luke

11:13). When we trust Christ for salvation, this promise is fulfilled in us, for Paul teaches that "if anyone does not have the Spirit of Christ, he does not belong to Christ" (Romans 8:9).

Improving Leadership

Hudson Taylor, founder of the China Inland Mission, was a simple yet astute man. He had the gift of saying tremendously significant things in a deceptively simple way. In a letter dated 1879 to the secretary of the mission, Taylor said:

> *The all-important thing to do is to*
> 1. *Improve the character of the work*
> 2. *Deepen the piety, devotion and success of the workers*
> 3. *Remove stones of stumbling, if possible*
> 4. *Oil the wheels where they stick*
> 5. *Amend whatever is defective*
> 6. *Supplement, as far as may be, what is lacking*

Such simple advice reveals insight into a leader's responsibility. Let's expand and apply. The leader must care for:

Administration—To improve the character of the work. The leader must discover which departments are functioning below standards and remedy the defect. This may involve new job descriptions, or establishing new reporting procedures and other lines of communication.

Spiritual tone—To deepen the piety, devotion, and success of the worker. The tone of the church or mission will be a reflection of its leaders. Water rises to the level of its source. The spiritual health of the leadership group should be a primary concern among higher echelon leadership. Job satisfaction is also important. If leaders show their colleagues methods to improve success, their sense of fulfillment will be reflected in an improvement in the quality of their work.

Group morale—To remove stones of stumbling. Friction among a team should be minimized. When problems are neglected, morale drops and performance decreases. If the problem has a remedy, it should be put into place at once. If the problem is a person, the delinquent should be dealt with as soon as the facts are clear, and let the chips fall. Of course the problem or person should be treated with consideration and love, but the work of God cannot be sacrificed for the sake of keeping peace.

Personal relationships—To oil the wheels where they stick. Warm relationships among team members are vital. Some workers prefer to administer; others want to love people. Only the latter are leaders. In handling people, the oil can filled with love is much more effective than the acid bottle filled with cold directives.

Problem solving—To amend what is defective. One of the chief duties of leaders is to solve tough problems within the organization. Creating problems is easy; solving them is difficult. The leader must face the problem realistically, and follow through until the solution is reached.

Creative planning—To supplement what is lacking. Criticizing plans is easier than creating them. The leader must see the goal clearly, plan imaginatively, and employ tactics that lead to success. In this department there is always a short supply of people ready and qualified to perform.

One more matter for improving leadership potential: resist the idea of "leadership from the rear." True leadership is always out front—never from the rear or the sidelines. It was leadership from the rear that led Israel back into the wilderness.

Many churches and organizations are in a stalemate because leaders have submitted to a kind of blackmail from the rear. No dissident or reactionary element should be allowed to determine group policy against the consensus of the spiritual leaders.

FOR REFLECTION

A. In both chapters 13 and 14 Sanders used the term "nettle." On page 110 he used the phrase "grasp the nettle." What did he mean and how does it apply to leadership?

B. What are your personal challenges and delights in relating to leaders in your life?

C. Which one of Hudson Taylor's six "all-important" things to do (page 112) would make the biggest difference in the area where you are called to lead? Why?

15
THE COST OF
LEADERSHIP

Can you drink the cup I drink or be baptized with the baptism I am baptized with?

Mark 10:38

To aspire to leadership in God's kingdom requires us to be willing to pay a price higher than others are willing to pay. The toll of true leadership is heavy, and the more effective the leadership, the greater the cost.

Quinton Hogg, founder of the London Polytechnic Institute, devoted a fortune to the enterprise. Asked how much it had cost to build the great institution, Hogg replied, "Not very much, simply one man's life blood."[1]

That is the price of every great achievement, and it is not paid in a lump sum. Achievement is bought on the time-payment plan, with a new installment required each day. The drain on resources is continuous, and when payments cease, leadership wanes. Our Lord taught that we could not save ourselves in the task of offering salvation to others. When Jesus said, "For whoever wants to save his life will lose it, but whoever loses his life for me will find it" (Matthew 16:25), part of what He meant has to do with hoarding personal resources in the vain hope that they will preserve us.

Samuel Brengle wrote:

> *Spiritual power is the outpouring of spiritual life, and like all life, from that of the moss and lichen on the wall to that of the archangel before the throne, it is from God. Therefore those who aspire to leadership may pay the price, and seek it from God.*[2]

Self-Sacrifice

This part of the cost must be paid daily. A cross stands in the path of spiritual leadership, and the leader must take it up. "Jesus Christ laid down his life for us. And we ought to lay down our lives for our brothers" (1 John 3:16). To the degree the cross of Christ is across our shoulders and over our backs, so the resurrection life of Christ is manifest through us. No cross, no leadership. Paul declared, "I die every day" (1 Corinthians 15:31b).

"Whoever wants to be first must be slave of all. For even the Son of Man did not come to be served, but to serve, and to give his life as a ransom for many" (Mark 10:44–45). Each of the heroes of faith in Hebrews 11 was called to sacrifice as part of his or her service. Those who lead the church are marked by a willingness to give up personal preferences, to surrender legitimate and natural desires for the sake of God. Bruce Barton quotes a sign at a service station: "We will crawl under your car oftener and get ourselves dirtier than any of our competition."[3] That is the kind of service the Christian seeks to give.

Samuel Zwemer remarked that the only thing Jesus took pains to show after His resurrection were His scars.[4] On the Emmaus road His disciples recognized neither Him nor His message. Not until Jesus broke the bread and they possibly saw the scars did they know the person for who He was. When Jesus stood among His demoralized band in the upper room after the resurrection, He showed them "both his hands and [His] side."

Scars are the authenticating marks of faithful discipleship and true spiritual leadership. It was said of one leader, "He belonged to that class of early martyrs whose passionate soul made an early holocaust of the physical man."[5] Nothing moves people more than the print of the nails and the mark of the spear. Those marks are tests of sincerity that none can challenge, as Paul knew well. "Let no one cause me trouble," he wrote, "for I bear on my body the marks of Jesus" (Galatians 6:17).

> *Hast thou no scar?*
> *No hidden scar on foot, or side, or hand?*
> *I hear thee sung as mighty in the land,*
> *I hear them hail the bright ascendant star:*
> *Hast thou no scar?*
>
> *Hast thou no wound?*
> *Yet, I was wounded by the archers, spent.*
> *Leaned me against the tree to die, and rent*
> *By ravening beasts that compassed me, I swooned:*
> *Hast thou no wound?*
>
> *No wound? No scar?*
> *Yes, as the master shall the servant be,*
> *And pierced are the feet that follow Me;*
> *But thine are whole. Can he have followed far*
> *Who has no wound? No scar?*
>
> **Amy Carmichael**[6]

Paul described himself and his burden this way:

> *On every hand hard-pressed am I—yet not crushed!*
> *In desperate plight am I—yet not in despair!*
> *Close followed by pursuers—yet not abandoned by Him!*
> *Beaten to earth—yet never destroyed!*
> *Evermore bearing about in my body*
> *The imminence of such a death as Jesus died,*
> *So that the life, too, of Jesus might be shown forth*
> *In this body of mine*

Always, always while I yet live
Am I being handed over to death's doom
For Jesus' sake!
So that in this mortal flesh of mine, may be
Shown forth also
The very life of Jesus

2 Corinthians 4:8–11 A. S. Way

Loneliness

Nietzsche believed that life always gets harder toward the summit—the cold gets colder, the wind stronger, the burden of responsibilities heavier.[7]

Because the leader must always be ahead of his followers, he lives with a particular loneliness. Though he may be friendly, there are areas of life where he must walk alone. Though he may seek counsel and support from others, decisions come back to the leader alone. Dixon Hoste felt the loneliness when Hudson Taylor retired and placed the leadership of China Inland Mission on his shoulders. Said Hoste after the appointment: "And now I have no one, no one but God!" There he stood on the mount with his God.

We naturally enjoy and need the company of others, and want to share with others the heavy burden of responsibility and care. It is sometimes heartbreaking to make decisions that affect the lives of beloved fellow workers—and to make them alone. Moses paid the price for his leadership—alone on the mountain, alone on the plain, misunderstood and criticized.

The Old Testament prophets were lonely men. Enoch walked alone in a decadent society as he preached judgment. His compensation was the presence of God. Jonah was alone in vast Nineveh, a heathen city of a million souls. The loneliest preacher today is the person who has been entrusted with a prophetic message ahead of the times, a message that cuts across the temper of the age.

Gregarious Paul was a lonely man, misunderstood by friends, misrepresented by enemies, deserted by converts. How poignant are his words to Timothy: "You know that everyone in the province of Asia has deserted me" (2 Timothy 1:15).

"Most of the world's greatest souls have been lonely," wrote A. W. Tozer. "Loneliness seems to be the price a saint must pay for his saintliness." The leader must be a person who, while welcoming the friendship and support of all who offer it, has sufficient inner resources to stand alone—even in the face of stiff opposition to have "no one but God."

> *On without cheer of sister or of daughter,*
> *Yes, without stay of father or of son,*
> *Lone on the land, and homeless on the water,*
> *Pass I in patience till my work be done.*
>
> F. W. H. Meyers

Fatigue

"The world is run by tired men." Perhaps an overstatement, but there is a grain of reality here. The demands of leadership wear down the most robust person. But Christians know where to find renewal. "Therefore do not lose heart. Though outwardly we are wasting away, yet inwardly we are being renewed day by day" (2 Corinthians 4:16). Even Jesus grew weary in ministry and had to rest (John 4:6). Jesus felt depleted in power, inner resources tapped, when the needy woman touched His clothing (Mark 5:30). No lasting good can be accomplished without this expenditure of nervous energy and personal power.

The spirit of the welfare state does not produce leaders. If a Christian is not willing to rise early and work late, to expend greater effort in diligent study and faithful work, that person will not change a generation. Fatigue is the price of leadership. Mediocrity is the result of never getting tired.

To the secretary of the Church Missionary Society, Douglas Thornton wrote:

> *But I am weary! I have only written because I am too weary*
> *to be working now, and too tired to sleep. . . . I am getting*

prematurely old, they tell me, and doctors do not give me long
to live unless the strain is eased a bit. My wife is wearier than
I am. She needs complete rest a while. . . . Oh, that the church
at home but realized one half of the opportunities of today!
Will no one hear the call? Please do your best to help us.[8]

Here were tired missionary leaders grasping the swiftly passing opportunities of their day.

Criticism

"There is nothing else that so kills the efficiency, capability and initiative of a leader as destructive criticism. . . . It tends to hamper and undercut the efficiency of man's thinking process. It chips away at his self-respect and undermines his confidence in his ability to cope with his responsibilities."[9]

No leader lives a day without criticism, and humility will never be more on trial than when criticism comes.

In a letter to a young minister, Fred Mitchell once wrote:

I am glad to know that you are taking any blessing there may
be found in the criticism brought against you by _____,
in which case even his bitter attack will yield sweetness. It
does not matter what happens to us, but our reaction to what
happens to us is vital. You must expect more criticism, for this
comes with responsibility. It causes us to walk humbly with
God, and to take such action as God desires.[10]

Samuel Brengle, noted for his sense of holiness, felt the heat of caustic criticism. Instead of rushing to defend himself, he replied: "From my heart I thank you for your rebuke. I think I deserved it. Will you, my friend, remember me in prayer?" When another critic attacked his spiritual life, Brengle replied: "I thank you for your criticism of my life. It set me to self-examination and heart-searching and prayer, which always leads me into a deeper sense of my utter dependence on Jesus for holiness of heart, and into sweeter fellowship with Him."[11]

With such a response, criticism is turned from a curse into a blessing, from a liability into an asset.

Paul sought the favor of God, not of people. His hard work was not to please those around him (Galatians 1:10). Nor was Paul terribly disturbed by criticism. "I care very little if I am judged by you or by any human court. . . . It is the Lord who judges me" (1 Corinthians 4:3–4). Paul could afford to take lightly the comments and criticism of others, for his heart was owned by God (Colossians 3:22).

But link indifference to human opinion with a weak spiritual life, and the formula is disaster. The same independence from human opinion can be a valuable asset to the person whose life goal is the glory of God. Paul's ear was tuned to the voice of God, and human voices were faint by comparison. He was fearless of human judgment, because he was conscious of standing before a higher tribunal (2 Corinthians 8:21).

Rejection

The leader who follows high spiritual standards may find himself following his Master on the pathway of rejection, for "he came unto his own and his own received him not."

J. Gregory Mantle tells of a minister whose congregation refused to accept his message. The minister wanted to lead his people into green pastures and beside still waters, but they were unwilling. The ungodly habits of his choir brought things to a head, and the minister invited the choir to resign. That the choir did, and it also persuaded the congregation to remain silent during the singing on the following Sunday. The minister sang alone.

Finally at wit's end, God spoke to him. On a park bench, he saw a piece of torn newspaper, which he picked up to read these words: "No man is ever fully accepted until he has, first of all, been utterly rejected." The minister needed nothing more. He had been utterly rejected for Christ's sake, and his recognition of the fact was the start of a fruitful ministry. Rejected by people, he had been accepted by God.

When A. B. Simpson resigned a pastorate, he learned the meaning of "destitute, despised, forsaken." He surrendered a comfortable salary, a position as senior pastor in a great American city, and all claim to denominational help for his yet untried work. He had no following, no organization, no resources, a large family to support, and everyone close to him was predicting failure. He often said that he looked down upon the stone in the street for the sympathy denied him by friends he treasured.

"The rugged path of utter rejection was trodden without complaint, and with rejoicing. He knew that though he . . . was going through fire and water, it was the divinely appointed way to the wealthy place."[12] To such a place Simpson was led. At his death he had established five schools for the training of missionaries, hundreds of missionaries in sixteen lands, and many churches in the United States and Canada that exerted a spiritual influence beyond their numbers.

"Often the crowd does not recognize a leader until he has gone, and then they build a monument for him with the stone they threw at him in life."[13]

Pressure and Perplexity

We naively think that the more we grow as Christians, the easier it will be to discern the will of God. But the opposite is often the case. God treats the mature leader as a mature adult, leaving more and more to his or her spiritual discernment and giving fewer bits of tangible guidance than in earlier years. The resulting perplexity adds inevitably to a leader's pressure.

D. E. Hoste said to a friend:

> *The pressure! It goes on from stage to stage, it changes in every period of your life. . . . Hudson Taylor said how in his younger days, things came so clearly, so quickly to him. "But," he said, "now as I have gone on, and God has used me more and more, I seem often to be like a man going along in a fog. I do not know what to do."*[14]

But when the time came to act, God always responded to His servant's trust.

Cost to Others

People close to a leader pay a price too. Sometimes a heavier price. Fred Mitchell wrote to his children when he accepted the invitation to become British director of China Inland Mission:

> *I have had many a sorrow of heart, and it still remains one of my chief regrets that I have not been able to give myself to mother and you children more. The harvest is great and the labourers few, which means that there have been many calls upon me. I do not justify my negligence, but any sacrifice made by you for our dear Lord Jesus' sake has not been unrewarded.*[15]

It takes a leader to embark on a dangerous venture. It takes a leader to build for the kingdom. That's why Jesus' words were so passionate: count the cost; take up the cross (see Luke 14:25–33).

FOR REFLECTION

A. When you add up the costs of leadership, what total do you get? How will you arrange payment?
B. Of the costs listed in this chapter (self-sacrifice, loneliness, fatigue, criticism, rejection, pressure and perplexity, and cost to others), which do you consider the most difficult to bear? Why?
C. Who will share/is sharing the cost of leadership with you? How do you encourage and appreciate them?

16
RESPONSIBILITIES
OF LEADERSHIP

Besides everything else, I face daily the pressure of my concern for all the churches.

2 Corinthians 11:28

Service

Jesus defined leadership as service, and His definition applies whether a leader works in secular or church organizations. Field Marshal Montgomery said that his war experience taught him that the staff must serve the troops and that a good staff officer must serve his commander while remaining anonymous himself.

In his book *Training of the Twelve*, A. B. Bruce wrote: "In other kingdoms they rule, whose privilege it is to be ministered unto. In the Divine commonwealth, they rule who account it a privilege to minister."[1] John A. MacKay of Princeton maintained that "servant" is the essential image of the Christian religion. The Son of God became the servant of God in order to do the mission of God. That image provides the pattern for mission societies, churches, and individual believers to fulfill their God-given mission.

The true leader is concerned primarily with the welfare of others, not with his own comfort or prestige. He shows sympathy for the problems of others, but his sympathy fortifies and stimulates; it does not soften and make weak. A spiritual leader will always direct the confidence of others to the Lord. He sees in each emergency a new opportunity for helpfulness. When God chose a leader to succeed Moses, it was Joshua, the man who had proved himself a faithful servant (Exodus 33:11).

D. E. Hoste spoke about the secrets of Hudson, whom Hoste has followed in leadership of the China Inland Mission:

> *Another secret of his influence among us lay in his great sympathy and thoughtful consideration for the welfare and comfort of those about him. The high standard of self-sacrifice and toil which he ever kept before himself, never made him lacking in tenderness and sympathy toward those who were not able to go as far as he did in these respects. He manifested great tenderness and patience toward the failures of his brethren, and was thus able in many cases to help them reach a higher plane of devotion.*[2]

Applied Discipline

Discipline is yet another responsibility of the leader, a duty often unwelcome. The self-discipline that is one of the central characteristics of a leader will eventually be applied consciously or unconsciously to those around him or her. Some will imitate the leader's disciplined life while others must be directed into that lifestyle by discipline. Further, the effectiveness and longevity of any Christian society requires godly and loving discipline to maintain divine standards in doctrine, morals, and conduct. Leaders preserve the standards through loving discipline.

Paul describes the spirit required in leaders who exercise discipline. "Brothers, if someone is caught in a sin, you who are spiritual should restore him gently. But watch yourself, or you also may be tempted" (Galatians 6:1). The fundamental ingredient in all discipline is love. "Warn him as a brother" (2 Thessalonians 3:15). "I urge you, therefore, to reaffirm your love for him" (2 Corinthians 2:8). The person who has faced up to his or her own problems and weaknesses is best able to help another in a way both loving and firm. The spirit of meekness will achieve far more than the spirit of criticism.

Approaching a disciplinary situation, the leader must remember five guidelines: (1) first conduct a thorough and impartial inquiry; (2) then consider the overall benefit of the disciplinary action to the work and to the individual; (3) do all in the spirit of love—be considerate always; (4) always keep the spiritual restoration of the offender in view; (5) pray it through.

Guidance

Providing guidance is a third area of responsibility. The spiritual leader must know where he or she is going before presuming to lead others. The Chief Shepherd gave us the pattern. "When he has brought out all his own, he goes on ahead of them, and his sheep follow him because they know his voice" (John 10:4). "The ideal leader," said A. W. Tozer, "is one who hears the voice of God, and beckons on as the voice calls him and them." Paul gave this challenge to the Corinthian Christians: "Follow my example, as I follow the example of Christ" (1 Corinthians 11:1). Paul knew whom he was following, where he was going, and could challenge others to follow him there.

It is not easy to guide people, even mature Christians, who have strong opinions of their own. The leader cannot assert his will recklessly. Said D. E. Hoste:

> *In a mission like ours, those guiding its affairs must be*
> *prepared to put up with waywardness and opposition, and be*
> *able to desist from courses of action which, though they may*
> *be intrinsically sound and beneficial, are not approved by some*
> *of those affected. Hudson Taylor again and again was obliged*
> *either to greatly modify, or lay aside projects which were sound*
> *and helpful, but met with determined opposition, and so*
> *tended to create greater evils than those which might have been*
> *removed or mitigated by the changes in question. Later on, in*
> *answer to patient continuance in prayer, many of those projects*
> *were put into effect.*[3]

Initiative

A leader must initiate. Some leaders are more gifted at conserving gains than starting new ventures, for maintaining order than generating ardor. The true leader must be venturesome as well as visionary. He must be ready to jump-start as well as hold speed. Paul constantly took calculated risks, always carefully and with much prayer, but always reaching for what lay beyond.

The leader must either initiate plans for progress or recognize the worthy plans of others. He must remain in front, giving guidance and direction to those behind. He does not wait for things to happen but makes them happen. He is a self-starter, always on the lookout for improved methods, eager to test new ideas.

Robert Louis Stevenson called the attitude of safety and security "that dismal fungus."[4] Hudson Taylor took steps of faith that appeared to others as wildcat schemes. The greatest achievements in the history of missions have come from leaders close to God who took courageous, calculated risks.

More failure comes from an excess of caution than from bold experiments with new ideas. A friend who filled an important global post in Christian outreach recently remarked that when he surveyed his life, most of his failures came from insufficient daring. The wife of Archbishop Mowll said, "The frontiers of the kingdom of God were never advanced by men and women of caution."[5]

A leader cannot afford to ignore the counsel of cautious people, who can save a mission from mistakes and loss. But caution should not curb vision, especially when the leader knows God is in control.

To take responsibility willingly is the mark of a leader. Joshua was such a person. He did not hesitate to follow one of the greatest leaders of all history, Moses. Joshua had more reason than Moses to plead inadequacy, but Joshua did not repeat Moses' sin. Instead, he promptly accepted and set about the work.

When Elijah was taken up, Elisha did not flinch at stepping in. He accepted the authority conferred by the falling mantle and became a leader in his own right.

In each case these leaders were assured of their divine calling. Once that issue is settled, no one need hesitate to do what God has set before him or her.

Archbishop Benson lived in a different era, but his rules for life carry relevance today:

- Eagerly start the day's main work.
- Do not murmur at your busyness or the shortness of time, but buy up the time all around.
- Never murmur when correspondence is brought in.
- Never exaggerate duties by seeming to suffer under the load, but treat all responsibilities as liberty and gladness.
- Never call attention to crowded work or trivial experiences.
- Before confrontation or censure, obtain from God a real love for the one at fault. Know the facts; be generous is your judgment. Otherwise, how ineffective, how unintelligible or perhaps provocative your well-intentioned censure may be.
- Do not believe everything you hear; do not spread gossip.
- Do not seek praise, gratitude, respect, or regard for past service.
- Avoid complaining when your advice or opinion is not consulted, or having been consulted, set aside.
- Never allow yourself to be placed in favorable contrast with anyone.
- Do not press conversation to your own needs and concerns.
- Seek no favors, nor sympathies; do not ask for tenderness, but receive what comes.
- Bear the blame; do not share or transfer it.
- Give thanks when credit for your own work or ideas is given to another.[6]

FOR REFLECTION

A. This chapter surveys four central leadership responsibilities: service, applied discipline, guidance, and initiative. Which of these are you most prepared to carry out? How have you developed your abilities?

B. Which of these responsibilities strike you as the most awkward or uncomfortable? Why?

C. Read thoughtfully back through Archbishop Benson's leadership rules (at the end of the chapter). Put a "c" next to the ones you find convicting; put an "m" next to those you find motivating and instructive; and put an "e" by those you find most encouraging and affirming.

17
TESTS OF LEADERSHIP

God tested Abraham.

Genesis 22:1

Then Jesus was led by the Spirit into the
desert to be tempted by the devil.

Matthew 4:1

Everyone entrusted with spiritual authority can expect tests, temptations, and trials along the way. As difficult and inconvenient as these tests may be, they serve to purify and clarify leadership. The first chapter of James demonstrates that God allows, even plans, these experiences for our good and for our growth. Tests are meant to let us succeed, not fail. Tests display progress.

Compromise

Can we waive a principle to reach agreement? Lowering standards is always a backward step, and compromise nearly always requires it.

The epic contest between Moses and Pharaoh is a classic example of the temptation to compromise. When Pharaoh realized that Moses meant to lead the Hebrews out of Egypt, he used cunning and threats to frustrate him. "Worship God if you will," was his first overture, "but don't leave Egypt to do it." A modern equivalent would be: "Religion is okay, but don't be narrow about it. No need to let religion isolate you from the rest of the world."

When that approach failed, Pharaoh tried something else: "If you must go out of Egypt to worship, don't go far. Religion is fine, but no need to be fanatical about it. Stay as close to the world as you can."

Yet a third attempt played on natural affection: "Let the men go and worship, and the women and children stay here. If you must break with the world, don't force such a narrow lifestyle on everyone else in the family."

Pharaoh's last attempt was an appeal to greed: "Okay, go. But the flocks and herds stay. Don't let your odd religious commitments get in the way of business and prosperity."

With clear spiritual insight Moses cut through each evasion: "Not a hoof is to be left behind," he said (Exodus 10:26). So Moses passed with honors a great test of his leadership of God's people.

Ambition

All great leaders—Moses too—face this test. During Moses' absence on Mount Sinai, the people of Israel turned to idolatry, and God became very angry, saying, "I will strike them down with a plague and destroy them, but I will make you into a nation greater and stronger than they" (Numbers 14:12).

Already Moses had heard more than enough of the people's constant complaining and frequent dalliance with paganism. Why not accept this divine proposal as a way to give the people their due, and start afresh with a smaller group that Moses could certainly control.

What a test, from the mouth of God Himself. Instead of personal ambition, Moses showed selfless nobility, genuine concern for God's glory, and compassion for the misguided people. Not for a moment did the thought of self-aggrandizement enter his lofty mind. Through prayer, Moses saved the apostate nation from judgment.

The Impossible Situation

"How does this person face impossible situations?" John R. Mott would inquire as a way to separate leaders from followers. Mott encouraged leaders to deal with impossible tasks rather than easy ones in order to foster personal competence, teamwork, and faith. "I long since ceased to occupy myself with minor things that can be done by others," he said. A true leader steps forward in order to face baffling circumstances and complex problems.

Our own day presents leaders with difficult problems as never before. If leaders are to survive, they must view the difficult as commonplace, the complex as normal.

Moses faced an impossible situation when Israel reached the Red Sea. Behind them was the desert and Pharaoh's army; before them was water, and Israel had no boats. Moses was in a cul-de-sac, and the people were getting edgy. Complaints started flying as morale dropped: "Is it because there were no graves in Egypt that you have taken us away to die in the wilderness?"

Moses, great man of faith, stayed himself on God. His orders must have sounded like sheer fantasy in the ears of the nation, but in point of fact that crisis was a defining moment of his leadership.

"Do not fear!" he cried, against every good reason to fear.

"Stand by!" he cried, as Pharaoh sped toward them.

"See the salvation of the Lord!"

So on that strange and wonderful day, the people of Israel saw their God in action, their hopes affirmed, their enemies crushed. The bracing lesson is that God delights to lead people, and then, in response to their trust, to show them power that matches every impossible situation.

Hudson Taylor faced many hard situations in his career to win China for Christ. He counted three phases in most great tasks undertaken for God—impossible, difficult, done.

> *Have you come to the Red Sea place in your life,*
> *Where in spite of all you can do,*
> *There is no way out, there is no way back,*
> *There is no other way but through?*
> *Then wait on the Lord with a trust serene*
> *Till the night of your fear is gone;*
> *He will send the wind, He will heap the floods,*
> *When He says to your soul, "Go on."*

In the morning watch, 'neath the lifted cloud,
You shall see but the Lord alone,
When He leads you on from the place of the sea
To a land that you have not known;
And your fears shall pass as your foes have passed,
You shall no more be afraid;
You shall sing His praise in a better place,
A place that His hand has made.

Annie Johnson Flint[1]

Failure

Many people who appear to be at the height of their careers hide a great inner sense of failure. Alexander Maclaren, the great British preacher, delivered a wonderful address to a large crowd, but turned away overwhelmed with failure. "I must not speak on such an occasion again," he said.[2]

Were his expectations too high? Or did the devil bring him grief when he should have felt great joy?

How a leader handles failure (or simply feelings of failure) will set much of the agenda for the future. Peter appeared washed up as a leader after his denial of the Christ, but repentance and love reopened the door of opportunity, and Peter's leadership touched all the rest of Christendom. "Where sin abounded, grace did much more abound."

Most Bible characters met with failure, and survived. Even when the failure was immense, those that found leadership again refused to lie in the dust and bemoan their tragedy. In fact, their failure led to a greater conception of God's grace. They came to know the God of the second chance, and sometimes the third and fourth.

The historian James Anthony Froude wrote: "The worth of a man must be measured by his life, not by his failure under a singular and peculiar trial. Peter the apostle, though forewarned, three times denied his Master on the first alarm of danger; yet that Master, who knew his nature in its strength and in its weakness, chose him."[3]

Successful leaders have learned that no failure is final, whether his own failure or someone else's. No one is perfect, and we cannot be right all the time. Failures and even feelings of inadequacy can provoke humility and serve to remind a leader who is really in charge.

Jealousy

Most leaders at some time face the problem of a jealous rival. Even Moses encountered that test. Jealousy is a common weapon of the devil.

Moses' first such challenge came from within his own family, his sister and brother. They had apparently forgotten that without Moses' noble decision to lead the people out of Egypt, they and all the rest of Israel would still be living under the slave master's lash.

Miriam by this time was elderly and should have known better. She promoted gossip against Moses because of his marriage to an Ethiopian. Race hatred is not the sin of this century alone. Miriam resented the intrusion of a foreigner and drew the weakling Aaron into her rebellion.

Not content with second place, Miriam and Aaron, led by the devil, tried to remove Moses by a coup. They cloaked their treachery in piety: "Has the LORD spoken only through Moses? . . . Hasn't he also spoken through us?"

Moses was deeply wounded, but he said nothing to vindicate himself. His main concern was God's glory, not his own position or privilege. "Now Moses was a very humble man, more humble than anyone else on the face of the earth" (Numbers 12:3). Yet though Moses maintained a dignified silence, God would not allow such a challenge to the authority of His servant to go without response.

Because the offense was public, judgment and punishment would also be public. "When the cloud lifted from above the Ten, there stood Miriam—leprous, like snow," the record states (Numbers 12:10). Such a drastic punishment points to the gravity of her sin, and once again Moses' greatness shines. His only response was to pray for his sister, and God graciously responded in mercy.

The lesson for the leader is plain. The person who fills a role appointed by God need not worry about vindicating his or her work when rivals become jealous or treacherous. Such a leader is safe in the hands of a heavenly Protector. Indeed, God shows how safe with His ominous words to Miriam: "Why then were you not afraid to speak against my servant Moses?" (Numbers 12:8).

Moses faced a second challenge from Korah and his henchmen, noted for their jealousy of Moses and Aaron. Korah wondered why these special two should enjoy the privilege of high office? Were not others (himself for one) equally deserving and qualified?

Once again Moses refused to vindicate himself against their charges. God intervened, judgment was rendered, and Moses stood higher than ever while the people grew in fear of God.

God will defend the leaders He has chosen. He will honor, protect, and vindicate them. Leaders need not worry about defending their rights or their office.

FOR REFLECTION

A. How does the promise of tests and difficulties affect your attitude about being a leader? Is it a caution, a challenge, or a reason to avoid leadership?

B. Which of the tests in this chapter have you already faced? How did you do?

C. In considering the various tests Moses faced and his responses, which one has offered you the most immediate help?

18
THE ART OF
DELEGATION

He chose capable men from all Israel and made them leaders of the people. . . .
They served as judges for the people at all times.
The difficult cases they brought to Moses.

Exodus 18:25–26

One facet of leadership is the ability to recognize the special abilities and limitations of others, combined with the capacity to fit each one into the job where he or she will do best. To succeed in getting things done through others is the highest type of leadership. Dwight L. Moody, a shrewd judge of people, once said that he would rather put a thousand men to work than do the work of a thousand men.[1] D. E. Hoste said: "The capacity to appreciate the gifts of widely varying kinds of workers, and then to help them along the lines of their own personalities and workings, is the main quality for oversight in a mission such as ours."[2]

Thoughtful delegation will save the leader the frustrating experience of managing square pegs serving in round holes.

Delegation to others of responsibility, together with the authority to do the job, is not always relished by one who enjoys exercising the authority himself. He is glad to give the responsibility to others but reluctant to let the reins of power slip from his own hands. Also, some leaders feel threatened by brilliant subordinates and therefore are reluctant to delegate authority. Whatever the basic cause, failure to delegate authority is unfair to the subordinate and unlikely to prove satisfactory or effective. Such an approach tends to be interpreted as indicating a lack of confidence, and that does not promote the best cooperation, nor will it draw out the full abilities of those being trained for leadership. Failure to delegate is also a poor stewardship of human resources God has provided!

It is possible that the subordinate may not do the task as well as his superior, but experience proves that that is by no means necessarily the case. Given the chance, the younger person may do it better because he or she is better able to feel the pulse of contemporary life. But in any case, how is the younger leader to gain experience unless he or she has been delegated both the responsibility and authority for the task?

The degree to which a leader is able to delegate work is a measure of his success. A one-person office can never grow larger than the load one person can carry.

Failing to delegate, the leader is caught in a morass of secondary detail; it overburdens him and diverts his attention from primary tasks. People under him do not achieve their own potential. In some cases, insisting on doing a job oneself is a result of simple conceit.

Once a leader delegates, he should show utmost confidence in the people he has entrusted. A. B. Simpson trusted those in charge of the various schools he founded, leaving them free to exercise their own gifts.[3] If they failed, Simpson took it as a reflection of his own failed leadership, for he had selected them.

Subordinates perform better when they feel sure of the leader's support, whether a given project succeeds or fails, so long as they have acted within the bounds of their assignment. This confidence comes when responsibilities have been clearly defined in writing, to eliminate any misunderstandings. Failing to communicate clearly has led to many unhappy problems and unsatisfying outcomes.

Paul Super wrote of his association with John R. Mott:

One of my greatest resources these ten years in Poland is the
sense of his backing. My greatest pride is his belief in me.
Surely one of my greatest motives is to be worthy of his support
and to measure up to his expectations of me.[4]

One of the great biblical illustrations of the principle of delegation is the story of Jethro, father-in-law to Moses, recorded in Exodus 18.

Israel emerged from Egypt an unorganized horde of ex-slaves. By the time of Exodus 18, a new national spirit was developing. Jethro saw that Moses faced intolerably heavy burdens—he was dealing with problems from morning till night. Moses was the legislature; Moses was the judiciary; Moses was the executive branch of the new nation. His decisions were accepted by the people as God's will.

Jethro saw that Moses could not keep such a pace, and made two solid arguments for delegating some of the work. First, "you and these people who come to you will surely wear yourselves out. The work is too heavy for you; you cannot handle it alone" (Exodus 18:18). Moses was at his limit, probably beyond his limit, of physical and emotional resources. Second, the current method of problem solving was too slow, and people were getting impatient. Sharing authority would speed up legal action, and the people would go away satisfied (Exodus 18:23).

Then Jethro proposed a two-part plan. Moses would continue to teach spiritual principles and exercise legislative leadership. He would also decide the hard cases at court. But much of his work would be delegated to competent, trustworthy subordinates.

Jethro spoke wisely, for if Moses had succumbed under the strain, he would have left chaos behind—no one trained to lead, no one in charge of anything. Failure to make provision for the succession of leadership has spelled ruin for many missions and churches.

Moses followed Jethro's advice and realized several benefits. He was able to concentrate on the biggest problems. The latent talents of many around him were discovered. Those gifted men, who could have become his critics had Moses continued alone, were now allies facing a common challenge. People-problems were solved with efficiency. And Moses laid the groundwork for effective leadership after his death.

Jethro encouraged Moses by articulating a spiritual principle of timeless relevance. "If you do this and God so commands, you will be able to stand the strain" (Exodus 18:23). Jethro placed his advice under the authority of God. God takes all responsibility for enabling His servants to do their work. Some tasks others can do better, and these should be delegated. But even if these secondary tasks are not done perfectly, still delegation is the better part of wisdom. Moses was probably better at judging than any of the seventy associate judges he appointed, but had he persisted alone, his career would have been cut short.

Jethro's spiritual discernment comes through in the qualifications he puts forward for the selection of this cadre: men of ability, for their work is formidable; men of piety, for fear of God is the beginning of wisdom; men of honor, who would shun bribes and greed.

It is a big mistake to assume more duties than we can discharge. There is no virtue in doing more than our fair share of the work. We do well to recognize our limitations. Our Jethros can often discern, better than we can, the impact of all our duties, and we should listen to them. If we break natural law—humans must sleep as well as work, for example—we cannot be exempt from repercussions. If we succumb to human persuasion and take on more than we should, God will accept no responsibility for the outcome.

Missionary leadership must be ready to delegate responsibility to nationals the moment they give evidence of spiritual maturity. Then the missionary must stand by them, ready to help but reluctant to intervene, guiding the national through trial and error so that he or she might learn spiritual leadership as the missionary did. Delegating in this way fulfills the essential task of discovering, training, and using the latent talents of national Christian colleagues. In the earlier stages, a wise watchfulness is necessary, but interfering should be reserved for acute needs only. The sense of being watched destroys confidence.

When W. E. Sangster was appointed general secretary of the Home Mission Department of the Methodist Church in Britain, he divided labor between all his subordinates, assigned responsibilities, and offered supervision. He never regretted placing such trust. It was said of Sangster: "Perhaps his greatest grasp of leadership was knowing the importance of delegation and of choosing assistants with care. He was always a master of that art."[5]

Writing about the leader of a large missionary society, a member of his staff commented: "He had a great gift of leadership in that he never interfered with those who worked under him. Everyone was left to do his own work." Another member wrote, "He knew what people could do, and saw that they did it, leaving them to make the best of their opportunities, and investigating only if things went wrong."[6]

FOR REFLECTION

A. What have been your most beneficial experiences in receiving delegated responsibilities?

B. How well do you delegate? How and when has delegation improved your effectiveness as a leader?

C. Which people in your life might benefit if you began to delegate responsibilities and opportunities to them?

19
REPLACING
LEADERS

Moses my servant is dead. Now then, you and all these people, get ready
to cross the Jordan River into the land I am about to give to them. . . .
As I was with Moses, so I will be with you.

Joshua 1:2,5

The ultimate test of a person's leadership is the health of the organization when the organizer is gone. This truth was behind Gamaliel's counsel to fellow Pharisees: "Leave these men alone! Let them go! For if their purpose or activity is of human origin, it will fail. But if it is from God, you will not be able to stop these men" (Acts 5:38–39). A work inspired by God and built on spiritual principles will survive the shock of leadership change and may even prosper as a result.

We sometimes demean God by assuming that the death of a great leader takes God by surprise, or sends God into emergency action. Though we may feel shock and anxiety, we need not tremble for the ark of God. Christian leadership is different from the worldly sort. God selects and prepares leaders for the kingdom (Mark 10:40). No work of God will be left destitute until its purposes are achieved.

Great movements are often thrown into crisis at the death of a founder. Such crises need not be fatal, however. Lyman Beecher said that he despaired when the first secretary of the American Board of Missions died. Then another leader arose and did so well that Beecher felt despair again when the second secretary died. At last, when the third secretary proved himself competent, Beecher began to feel confident that God's resources were equal to the task at hand. When Beecher himself was gone, some believed he could not be replaced. But all of Beecher's causes—temperance, orthodoxy, and foreign missions—found capable new leaders in God's time and way.[1] Indeed, no man, however gifted and devoted, is indispensable to the work of the kingdom.

God is always at work, though we cannot see it, preparing people He has chosen for leadership. When the crisis comes, God fits His appointee into the place ordained for him. Often such a replacement is not apparent to an organization, but time will reveal him.

God's greatest gifts to Israel, better than the land itself, were men like Moses and David and Isaiah. God's greatest gifts are always the servants through whom He works. His greatest endowment to the church was the gift of twelve men trained for leadership.

Imagine how distraught were the Israelites when the time approached for Moses to leave them. For four decades the entire nation had looked to him for problem solving and direction. Moses had interpreted the will of God for them. True, seventy elders served under him, but there was not another Moses. Adding to the sense of crisis was the timing of his death, just at the point of entry in Canaan. The people could hardly believe that God had a new leader in reserve. But Joshua was in preparation, and the crisis brought him to the fore.

This situation is repeated throughout history; each generation learns the same lesson. The loss of an outstanding leader awakens doubts and fears. What will the Methodists do without Wesley? What will the Salvation Army do without Booth? What will our church do when the pastor moves?

The paths of glory lead always to the grave, but a new glory will be revealed. The greatest leader must inevitably be removed by death or some other cause, and the sense of loss will vary with the caliber of his leadership. But in retrospect it will usually be seen that the seeming tragedy has actually turned out to be in the best interests of the work.

Only after his removal are the character and achievements of a leader fully revealed. It was not until after Moses' death that Israel saw his greatness in the light of his completed work. "The emphasis of death makes perfect the lessons of the life."

At the same time, a leader's passing cuts his persona down to size in relation to the work of God. However great his achievements, no one is indispensable. The time comes when his special contribution is not the need of the hour. The most gifted leader has liabilities and limitations that become apparent when a successor comes along to advance the work. Often a successor with less fame and prestige than a founder is better able to develop the work because of the specific gifts he has. We must assume that Joshua was better equipped to conquer Canaan than Moses.

The departure of a strong and dominating leader makes room for others to emerge and develop. Often when the weight of responsibility falls suddenly on his shoulders, a subordinate develops abilities and qualities he and others had not suspected he had. Joshua would never have developed into an outstanding leader had he remained one of Moses' lieutenants.

A shift in leadership also provides occasion for God to show His versatility in adjusting means to ends. His resources in any work He initiates are inexhaustible. If a man who possesses great gifts will not place them at the disposal of God, He is not defeated. God will take a man of lesser gifts that are fully available to Him and will supplement those gifts with His own mighty power. Paul implied this when he wrote to the Corinthians, 1 Corinthians 1:26–29:

> Brothers, think of what you were when you were called. Not many of you were wise by human standards; not many were influential; not many were of noble birth. But God chose the foolish things of the world to shame the wise; God chose the weak things of the world to shame the strong. He chose the lowly things of this world and the despised things—and the things that are not—to nullify the things that are, so that no one may boast before him.

God is surely eager to use the powers of naturally gifted people, but few of them are as willing as was Paul to place those gifts without reservation at God's disposal. When such people learn to rely not on their own power and wisdom but to depend on God, there is no limit to their usefulness in God's service.

Toward the end his life, A. B. Simpson was at a great convention when a respected New York minister observed that there was no one similarly qualified to continue leadership of the organization when Simpson's tenure was done. The minister suggested that a large endowment be established to ensure that the work continue. Simpson said nothing and did nothing. He believed that if his work was from God, nothing could dismantle it; if it were not from God, no good purpose was served by keeping it going.[2]

How Simpson rejoiced during the last months of his life, when he had retired from leadership in the Alliance, as reports came in of increased missionary offerings and progress on the foreign fields. The year after his death proved to be the most prosperous year in the history of the society to that date. No greater tribute could be paid to the quality of Simpson's leadership.

Only one Leader holds office forever; no successor is needed for Him. The disciples made no move to appoint a replacement for Jesus, tacit evidence that they were conscious of His abiding presence, their living leader and Lord. At times the church has lost a vivid sense of Jesus' presence, but there has never been a panic cry from a leaderless army. The perils and distress of the church weigh deeply on Jesus' heart.

"We tell our Lord plainly," said Martin Luther, "that if He will have His Church then He must look to and maintain and defend it, for we can neither uphold nor protect it; and if we could, then we should become the proudest donkeys under heaven."

Since our Leader conducts His work in the power of an endless life— He is the same yesterday, today, and forever—changes in human leadership should not shake or dismay us.

FOR REFLECTION

A. Who's easier to replace—an ineffective or an effective leader? Why?

B. Explain how you agree or disagree with this statement: Great leaders may be replaced but their effect can't be erased.

C. What are the first crucial steps to take when you have to fill someone else's big shoes?

20
REPRODUCING
LEADERS

The things you have heard me say in the presence of many witnesses
entrust to reliable men who will also be qualified to teach others.

2 Timothy 2:2

With the words above Paul presses home a leader's responsibility to train others to lead. If he is to carry out his trust fully, the leader will devote time to training others to succeed and perhaps even supercede him. Barnabas's spiritual stature is seen in his entire freedom from jealousy when his protégé Paul surpassed his own leadership skills and became the dominant member of the team. It follows that a leader must provide subordinates with opportunity to exercise and develop their powers.

John R. Mott believed that leaders must multiply themselves by growing younger leaders, giving them full play and adequate outlet for their abilities. Younger people should feel the weight of heavy burdens, opportunity for initiative, and power of final decision. The younger leader should receive generous credit for achievements. Foremost they must be trusted. Blunders are the inevitable price of training leaders.

At a recent missionary conference, an Asian leader spoke frankly about the role of Western missionaries: "The missionary of today in the Orient should be less a performer, and more a trainer." This may not be true in every missionary setting, but it does highlight one of the great needs in current mission strategy.

Training new leaders is a delicate task. The wise trainer will not advertise the end he has in view. Bishop Stephen Neill spoke of the danger of this task:

> *If we set out to produce a race of leaders, what we shall succeed in doing is probably to produce a race of restless, ambitious and discontented intellectuals. To tell a man he is called to be a leader is the best way of ensuring his spiritual ruin, since in the Christian world ambition is more deadly than any other sin, and, if yielded to, makes a man unprofitable in the ministry. The most important thing today is the spiritual, rather than the intellectual, quality of those indigenous Christians who are called to bear responsibility in the younger churches.*

Lesslie Newbigin goes so far as to question whether the church ought to encourage the concept of leadership, so difficult it is to use without being confused with its non-Christian counterpart. The church needs saints and servants, not "leaders," and if we forget the priority of service, the entire idea of leadership becomes dangerous. Leadership training must still follow the pattern our Lord used with His twelve.[1]

Perhaps the most strategic and fruitful work of modern missionaries is to help leaders of tomorrow develop their spiritual potential. This task requires careful thought, wise planning, endless patience, and genuine Christian love. It cannot be haphazard, hurried, or ill conceived. Our Lord devoted the greater part of His three years of ministry to molding the characters and spirits of His disciples.

Paul showed the same concern for training young Timothy and Titus. Paul's method for preparing Timothy for the church in Ephesus is deeply instructive.

Timothy was about twenty years old when Paul became his friend. Timothy tended toward melancholia, and he was too tolerant and partial to people of rank. He could be irritable with opponents. He was apt to rely on old spiritual experiences rather than kindle the flame of daily devotion.

But Paul had high hopes for him. Paul set about to correct Timothy's timid nature, to replace softness with steel. Paul led Timothy into experiences and hardships that toughened his character. Paul did not hesitate to assign him tasks beyond his present powers. How else can a young person develop competence and confidence if not by stretching to try the impossible?[2]

Traveling with Paul brought Timothy into contact with men of stature whose characters kindled in him a wholesome ambition. From his mentor he learned to meet triumphantly the crises that Paul considered routine. Paul shared with Timothy the work of preaching. Paul gave him the responsibility of establishing a group of Christians at Thessalonica. Paul's exacting standards, high expectations, and heavy demands brought out the best in Timothy, saving him from a life of mediocrity.

Paul Rees describes the experience of Douglas Hyde, onetime communist but later a convert to Christ, as recorded in Hyde's book, *Dedication and Leadership Techniques*:

> *Easily one of the most fascinating stories in the book—a story connected with his Communist years—involves a young man who came to Hyde and announced that he wanted to be made into a leader. "I thought," said Hyde, "I had never seen anyone look less like a leader in my life. He was short, grotesquely fat, with a great, flabby, wide uninteresting face. . . . He had a cast in one eye, and spoke with a most distressing stutter."*
>
> *What happened? Well, instead of turning him away as a hopeless prospect, Hyde gave him a chance—a chance to study, to learn, to test his dedication, to smooth out his stutter. In the end he became a leader in one of the most Communist-infiltrated labour unions in Britain.[3]*

The observant leader may discover latent talent in some quite unpromising people.

Frank Buchman, founder of Moral Rearmament, displayed many leadership gifts. He claimed that if he failed to train others to do his work better than he did it, he had failed. For many years he worked to make himself dispensable, a rare agenda for a founder.[4]

No work is more rewarding to a missionary than developing leaders, for the survival and health of the new churches the missionary plants will greatly depend on the spiritual caliber of the national Christians. Once the pioneer stage in any field has passed, the training of leadership should take high priority. One of a missionary's main goals should be the development of faith in promising young people who can, in time, lead the church.

Lest our training programs become too rigid and we discourage the exceptional person from service, we must always allow room for the unusual person, the one for whom there is no mold. God has His "irregulars," and many of them have made outstanding contributions to world evangelization. Who could have poured C. T. Studd into a mold? Such men and women cannot be measured by ordinary standards or made to conform to any fixed pattern.

One such missionary was Douglas Thornton, who made an indelible mark among Muslims in the Near East. He possessed rare gifts, and even as a young man did not hesitate to express opinions that seemed radical and impractical to his superiors. His biographer records:

> It is hardly surprising to learn that he felt constrained to
> write to his society a memorandum setting forth his views
> on the past, present and future of the work in Egypt. It is
> not a precedent that young missionaries after three and a
> half months on the field should be invited to follow, and on
> this occasion, too, heads were shaken. But Thornton was an
> exceptional man, and time has proven that his views and even
> his effusions were worthy of being studied. It was never safe to
> neglect them. Most juniors had best reserve their observations
> for a more mature season. But when the exceptional man
> arrives, two things have to be observed—the man has to learn
> to make his observations in the right way, so as to carry his

seniors with him; the seniors have to learn how to learn from one who is possibly able, in spite of his want of local knowledge, to benefit them enormously by his fresh and spontaneous ideas. Each is a difficult lesson.[5]

Leadership training cannot be done on a mass scale. It requires patient, careful instruction and prayerful, personal guidance over a considerable time. "Disciples are not manufactured wholesale. They are produced one by one, because someone has taken the pains to discipline, to instruct and enlighten, to nurture and train one that is younger."

When a person is really marked out for leadership, God will see that that person receives the necessary disciplines for effective service.

> *When God wants to drill a man*
>   *And thrill a man*
>   *And skill a man,*
> *When God wants to mold a man*
>   *To play the noblest part;*
> *When He yearns with all His heart*
>   *To create so great and bold a man*
> *That all the world shall be amazed,*
>   *Watch His methods, watch His ways!*
> *How He ruthlessly perfects*
>   *Whom He royally elects!*
> *How He hammers him and hurts him,*
>   *And with mighty blows converts him*
> *Into trial shapes of clay which*
>   *Only God understands;*
> *While his tortured heart is crying*
>   *And he lifts beseeching hands!*
> *How He bends but never breaks*
>   *When his good He undertakes;*
> *How He uses whom He chooses*
>   *And with every purpose fuses him;*
>   *By every act induces him*

To try His splendour out—
God knows what He's about!

Author unknown

FOR REFLECTION

A. How do delegation (chapter 18) and leadership reproduction work together in shaping a leader?

B. Why does leadership reproduction need to be person to person rather than in a group setting? Who initiates a leadership reproduction relationship?

C. How have others been involved in reproducing and encouraging leadership capabilities in you?

21
PERILS OF
LEADERSHIP

. . . so that after I have preached to others,
I myself will not be disqualified for the prize.

1 Corinthians 9:27

The perils of spiritual leadership are especially subtle, more so than for other callings. The leader is not immune from temptations of the flesh, but the greater dangers are in the realm of spirit, for the enemy Satan never fails to exploit the advantage in any area of weakness.

Pride

When a person rises in position, as happens to leaders in the church, the tendency to pride also increases. If not checked, the attitude will disqualify the person from further advancement in the kingdom of God, for "the LORD detests all the proud of heart" (Proverbs 16:5). These are strong and searching words! Nothing aggravates God more than conceit, the sin that aims at setting the self upon a throne, making of God a secondary figure. That very sin changed the anointed cherub into the foul fiend of hell.

Pride takes many forms, but spiritual pride is the most grievous. To become proud of spiritual gifts or leadership position is to forget that all we have is from God, and that any position we occupy is by God's appointment.

The victim of pride is often least aware of the sin. Three tests help us identify the problem:

The test of precedence. How do we react when another is selected for the position we wanted to fill? When another is promoted in our place? When another's gifts seem greater than our own?

The test of sincerity. In our moments of honest self-reflection, we often admit to problems and weaknesses. How do we feel when others identify the same problems in us?

The test of criticism. Does criticism lead to immediate resentment and self-justification? Do we rush to criticize the critic?

When we measure ourselves by the life of Jesus, who humbled Himself on the cross, we are overwhelmed with the shabbiness, even the vileness, of our hearts, and we cry:

> *Boasting excluded, pride I abase;*
> *I'm only a sinner, saved by grace.*
>
> James M. Gray

Egotism

One of the repulsive manifestations of pride, egotism is the practice of thinking and speaking of oneself, of magnifying one's attainments and relating everything to the self rather than to God and God's people. The leader who has long enjoyed the admiration of many followers stands in peril of this danger.

When Robert Louis Stevenson arrived in Samoa, he was invited to address students training for the pastorate at the Malua Institute. His talk was based on the Muslim story of the veiled prophet, a brilliant teacher who wore a veil because, he claimed, the glory of his presence was too great for men to bear the sight.

At last the veil grew ragged and fell off. Then the people discovered that the brilliant prophet was only an decrepit old man trying to hide his ugliness. Stevenson went on to make the point that, however grand the truths a preacher taught, however skillful the outward image of the leader, the time comes when the veil falls away and a man is seen by the people as he really is. Will the leader reflect the ugliness of egotism or the transfigured glory of Christ the Lord?

> *It is a good test to the rise and fall of egotism to notice how you listen to the praises of other men of your own standing. Until you can listen to the praises of a rival without any desire to indulge in detraction or any attempt to belittle his work, you may be sure there is an unmortified prairie of egotistic impulse in your nature yet to be brought under the grace of God.* [1]

Jealousy

This near relative of pride describes the person who is envious of rivals. Moses faced such a temptation through the loyalty of his own colleagues. When Eldad and Medad were "prophesying in the camp," an outraged Joshua reported, "Moses, my lord, stop them!" (Numbers 11:27–28).

But the great leader saw the situation for what it was, an outbreak of God's Spirit among the assistants Moses had selected. "Are you jealous for my sake?" Moses replied to Joshua. "I wish that all the LORD's people were prophets" (Numbers 11:29). Envy and jealousy found no fertile ground in Moses' heart. God's work in others was to be encouraged, not snuffed out.

Popularity

What leader or preacher does not desire to be liked by his people? Being disliked is no virtue, but popularity can have too high a price. "Woe unto you when all men speak well of you," Jesus warned.

Personality cults have often developed around great spiritual leaders. Followers are awestruck at a leader's virtues, and show such fawning deference that the leader seems no longer merely human. Worse yet, sometimes the leader comes to enjoy his pedestal.

Paul faced this problem at Corinth. Christians there were splintering into camps promoting their favorite: some liked Apollos, others liked Paul. The apostle saw the danger and immediately put a stop to it. Neither of them warranted such favoritism, "but only God" (1 Corinthians 3:7). Any fervor, devotion, or loyalty the people in Corinth might have for spiritual leaders should be fastened tightly to the person of Jesus.

Spiritual leaders may be "esteemed highly in love for their work's sake," but esteem that becomes adulation has degenerated. Leaders must work to attach the people's affection to Jesus. There is no fault in finding encouragement when one's service is appreciated, but the leader must altogether refuse to be idolized.

Stephen Neill said in a lecture to theological students: "Popularity is the most dangerous spiritual state imaginable, since it leads on so easily to the spiritual pride which drowns men in perdition. It is a symptom to be watched with anxiety since so often it has been purchased at the too heavy price of compromise with the world."[2]

Spurgeon also felt the danger of popularity pressing close to his heart:

> *Success exposes a man to the pressure of people and thus tempts him to hold on to his gains by means of fleshly methods and practices, and to let himself be ruled wholly by the dictatorial demands of incessant expansion. Success can go to my head, and will unless I remember that it is God who accomplished the work, that He can continue to do so without any help, and that He will be able to make out with other means whenever He cuts me down to size.*[3]

George Whitefield was immensely popular, and in his early years he enjoyed the acclaim. He recalled that he felt it was death to be despised and worse than death to be laughed at. But as his service and career progressed, he grew tired of the attention. "I have seen enough of popularity to be sick of it," he declared.

Infallibility

Spirituality does not guarantee infallible judgment. The Spirit-filled person is less likely to make mistakes of judgment than his secular counterpart, but perfection eludes us all, whatever our level of spiritual development. Even the apostles made mistakes that required divine correction.

Spiritual leaders who have given such a significant share of their lives to knowing God, to prayer, and to wrestling with the problems of renewal and revival may find it difficult to concede the possibility of misjudgment or mistake. Surely the leader must be a person of strength and decisiveness, to stand for what he believes. But willingness to concede error and to defer to the judgment of one's peers increases one's influence rather than diminishes it. Followers will lose confidence in a leader who appears to believe himself to be infallible. It is strange but true that a high level of genuine authority in one area of life often coexists with great humility in other areas.

Indispensability

Many influential Christians have fallen before this temptation. It seems that Christians are especially prone to it. They cling to authority long after it should have passed to younger people. The author met a wonderful Christian in his nineties who was still superintendent of his church's Sunday school. Younger people were willing and available, but no one in the church had been able to approach this saint about retirement. One unfortunate consequence is that young people who have energy to fill a role are held back and stagnate.

Sometimes sincere and well-meaning followers encourage the notion of indispensability, which feeds a leader's ego and makes him even less objective about performance in office. And we do become less objective about our work as we get older.

The missionary who has raised a church to believe that he is indispensable has done the church an injustice. From the earliest days of the work, the missionary should be planning on working out of a job. National leadership needs to learn how to depend on the Lord, how to train its own spiritual leaders, and how to take responsibility for the work.

Elation and Depression

Every work of God includes days of frustration and days of joy. The leader is in peril of becoming overly depressed by the one and overly elated by the other. Discovering the balance here is not easy.

When the seventy disciples returned from their mission elated with results, Jesus checked their euphoria. "Do not rejoice that the spirits submit to you, but rejoice that your names are written in heaven" (Luke 10:20).

After the drama at Carmel (1 Kings 18), Elijah was so depressed that he wanted to die. The Lord corrected his self-pity in a most common manner, by insisting on two long sleeps and two decent meals. Only then did the spiritual lessons begin, and they made a lifelong difference to Elijah. His discouragement was unfounded: seven thousand faithful Israelites had not yet bowed to Baal. By running away, Elijah had deprived this remnant of leadership they desperately needed.

Not all our ideals and goals for the work of God will be realized. People we trust will disappoint us; cherished plans will fall victim to shortfalls or sickness; the sacrifices leaders make will be interpreted as selfish gestures. Bad things happen, but the spiritual leader should discern the reasons for depression and deal with it accordingly.

F. B. Meyer was an eternal optimist, ever hopeful, ever vigorous, ever confident of the triumph of good over evil. But he was also

> *far too keen and thoughtful a man . . . not to be overcome now and again by the pessimistic views of life. He occasionally went down into the very depths of human despair. He had seen too often and too clearly the seamy side of life not to be sad and pessimistic now and then.*[4]

Another kind of depression is described by Spurgeon in his lecture, "The Minister's Fainting Fits":

> *Before any great achievement, some measure of depression is very usual. . . . Such was my experience when I first became a pastor in London. My success appalled me, and the thought of the career which seemed to open up so far from elating me, cast me into the lowest depth, out of which I muttered my* miserere *and found no room for a* gloria in excelsis. *Who was I that I should continue to lead so great a multitude? I would betake me to my village obscurity, or emigrate to America and find*

*a solitary nest in the backwoods where I might be sufficient
for the things that were demanded of me. It was just then the
curtain was rising on my lifework, and I dreaded what it might
reveal. I hope I was not faithless, but I was timorous and filled
with a sense of my own unfitness. . . . This depression comes
over me whenever the Lord is preparing a larger blessing for my
ministry.*[5]

Seasons there are when all goes well. Goals are reached, plans find
success, the Spirit moves, souls are saved, and saints blessed. When
Robert Murray McCheyne went through times like this, he would kneel
down and symbolically place the crown of success on the brow of the
Lord, to whom it rightly belonged. That habit helped save him from
assuming the glory for achievement that belonged to God alone.

Samuel Chadwick wisely said: "If successful, don't crow; if defeated
don't croak."[6]

Prophet or Leader?

Sometimes we come to a fork in the path, and both ways look good
and true. For example, a preacher with gifts of leadership faces a decision whether to be a popular leader or unpopular prophet. A. C. Dixon
faced such a dilemma:

*Every preacher ought to be primarily a prophet of God who
preaches as God bids him, without regard to results. When he
becomes conscious of the fact that he is a leader in his own
church or denomination, he has reached a crisis in his ministry.
He must now choose one of two courses, that of prophet of God
or a leader of men. If he seeks to be a prophet and a leader, he
is apt to make a failure of both. If he decides to be a prophet
only insofar as he can do without losing his leadership, he
becomes a diplomat and ceases to be a prophet at all. If he
decides to maintain leadership at all costs, he may easily fall to
the level of a politician who pulls the wires in order to gain or
hold a position.*[7]

Dixon maximizes the differences between leader and prophet; in reality, however, the roles overlap. But situations develop in which a leader must choose between the hellfire of prophetic warning and the gentle prodding of pastoral work. Herein lies the peril.

Reuben A. Torrey, whom God used at the turn of the century to bring revival to half the world, faced such a choice. Dixon wrote of him:

> *The thousands who have heard Dr. Torrey know the man and his message. He loves the Bible, and believing it to be the infallible Word of God, preaches it with the fervor of red-hot conviction. He never compromises. He has chosen to be a prophet of God rather than a mere leader of men, and that is the secret of his power with God and men.*[8]

Disqualification

Despite his success as a missionary and leader, Paul was never without a wholesome, watchful fear that he himself might be disqualified (1 Corinthians 9:27). To him this prospect was an ever-present warning against smugness and complacency. So should it be to all who are entrusted with spiritual responsibility.

The Greek work for "disqualified" (in other translations "castaway" or "disapproved") in verse 27 is used of metals that were not suitable for coinage. These metals could not survive the test; the refining process had left them below standard. Paul refers here to losing the coveted prize for failure to comply with the rules of the contest.

Paul's metaphor puts him in two roles here. He is a competitor in the context, and also the herald who announces the rules of the game and calls runners to the starting line. Paul feared that after acting as a herald (preaching), he himself should fail by the very standards he preaches. In that case, his position as herald would only serve to aggravate his own guilt, shame, and disgrace.

The failure before Paul's eyes here is failure of the body, and to guard against it requires rigorous self-discipline. Charles Hodge affirms that in Scripture the body is "the seat and organ of sin, and refers to our whole sinful nature. It was not merely his sensual nature Paul endeavored to bring into subjection, but all the evil propensities of his heart."[9]

Paul believed he could be disqualified not merely because of errors of doctrine or misjudgments of ethics but because of the body's passions. Paul worked toward mastering the body's appetites through disciplined moderation—neither asceticism on the one hand (such as causing oneself harm by denial of basic needs) nor self-indulgence on the other (losing strength through careless diet, for example). Paul was not willing to give in to bodily appetites, as if they were his master. He insisted on being in command of his own bodily needs and wants. A. S. Way rendered this passage: "I browbeat my own animal nature, and treat it not as my master but my slave."

FOR REFLECTION

A. Chapter 17 highlighted the tests of leadership. This chapter has surveyed the parallel perils of leadership. What warnings do you find in this chapter about possible hidden dangers behind successes and effectiveness in a leader?

B. The section on pride includes a three-part test for self-diagnosing pride. If you haven't submitted to the tests, take a few minutes to ask yourself those questions.

C. In what ways can you relate to the apostle Paul's concern about personal disqualification?

22
THE LEADER
NEHEMIAH

Remember me with favor, O my God.

Nehemiah 13:31

Nehemiah is one of the most inspiring leaders in the Bible. At times his methods seem somewhat vigorous, but they were used by God to achieve spectacular reforms in the life of his nation in an amazingly short time. An analysis of his personality and methods discloses that the methods he adopted were effective only because of the quality of his character.

His Character

The first impression a reader gains from this straightforward story is that Nehemiah was a man of prayer. For Nehemiah prayer was an ordinary part of living and working. Prayer was his first reaction on hearing the plight of emigrants in Jerusalem. Nehemiah was no stranger at the throne of grace (Nehemiah 1:4,6; 2:4; 4:4,9; 5:19; 6:14; 13:14,22,29).

He showed courage in the face of danger. "Should a man like me run away? Or should one like me go into the temple to save his life?

I will not go" (Nehemiah 6:11). Such firm fearlessness would inspire any discouraged people.

His genuine concern for the welfare of others was so obvious that even his enemies noticed (Nehemiah 2:10). He expressed his concern in fasting, prayer, and tears (Nehemiah 1:4–6). Nehemiah identified with his people in their sorrows and in their sins: "I confess the sins we Israelites, including myself and my father's house, have committed against you" (Nehemiah 1:6).

Nehemiah exhibited keen foresight. He knew that opposition was sure to arise, so he secured letters from the king for safe passage and for the resources to accomplish the task, "to make beams for the gates of the citadel . . . and for the city wall" (Nehemiah 2:8). He carefully planned his strategy.

Through all his adventures and boldness, there runs a strain of caution. He did not jump into the work immediately upon arrival but waited three days to appraise the situation (Nehemiah 2:11). And when he did set to business, he did not hold a tell-all press conference but kept his goals largely secret, even doing reconnaissance under cover of night.

Nehemiah could make clear decisions. He did not put off the tough call but cut to the heart and made a judgment. And his decisions were impartial; he did not play favorites. When censure was needed, he gave it to officials and executives as well as to workers (Nehemiah 5:7).

Nehemiah was uncommonly empathetic. He listened to grievances and took remedial action (Nehemiah 4:10–12; 5:1–5). He let people "weep on his shoulder." He sympathized with others.

Nehemiah was a realist; he understood the mechanics of the real world. "We prayed to our God and posted a guard day and night" (Nehemiah 4:9).

He accepted responsibility with the intention of following through on all assignments, the pleasant ones and the dirty ones, until the job was done.

Nehemiah was a vigorous administrator, a calm crisis manager, a fearless initiator, a courageous decision maker, and a persevering leader. He was resolute in the face of threats and vigilant against treachery—a leader who won and held the full confidence of his followers.

His Methods

Nehemiah raised the morale of his colleagues, an important part of any leader's work. He built up their faith by redirecting focus away from "the impossible" toward the greatness of God. Throughout the record are such assurances as "the God of heaven will give us success" (Nehemiah 2:20) and "the joy of the LORD is your strength" (Nehemiah 8:10).

Faith builds faith. Pessimism dismantles faith. The spiritual leader's primary task is to build the faith of others.

Nehemiah encouraged others generously. When he arrived, the people were demoralized. First, he kindled hope by testifying to the vision and providence of God, and then secured their cooperation. "I told them about the gracious hand of my God upon me and what the king had said to me. They replied, 'Let us start building.' So they began this good work" (Nehemiah 2:18).

Faults and failures must be corrected, but method makes all the difference. Nehemiah could point to people's shortcomings and find hope for a better day. Then his great personal discipline convinced the people that his optimism wasn't mere giddiness but the strength of deep conviction. And so he won their confidence and established his authority.

Nehemiah promptly faced potential weaknesses in the plan. Two cases illustrate.

The people were discouraged and tired. Opponents were making life miserable (Nehemiah 4:10–16). Garbage was piling up and hampering progress. Nehemiah first directed their vision to God, then put them under arms and deployed them at strategic points. He harnessed the strength of the family unit, ordering half a family to work while the other half stood guard and rested. The people recovered their courage as Nehemiah solved real problems through decisive action.

In the second instance the people were disillusioned by the greed of their own rich brothers (Nehemiah 5:1–15). Most people lived on mortgaged land; some had sold children as slaves to meet expenses. "Neither is it in our power to redeem them; for other men have our lands and vineyards" (Nehemiah 5:5 KJV). What an awkward mess: children of "have-nots," victims of an economy where wealth was held in the hands of a few, and those few were not about to release their grasp.

Nehemiah listened to their stories and sympathized with their suffering. He rebuked the nobles for their heartless usury (Nehemiah 5:7) and appealed for immediate relief (Nehemiah 5:11). So effective was his negotiation that the reply of the nobles was simply, "We will do as you say" (Nehemiah 5:12).

Nehemiah recovered the authority of the Word of God in the lives of the people (Nehemiah 8:1–8). Without the standard of God's Word, all the work would be for naught. What does success matter if we have no standard, no vision of ultimate goals, no purpose larger than laying bricks on bricks? Nehemiah's greatest gift to the people was to show them why all this work was important. He restored the Feast of Tabernacles, which had not been observed since Joshua's day. He led the people to repentance through the reading of the law (Nehemiah 9:3–5). He purified the temple of pagan influence (Nehemiah 13:4–9). He encouraged tithing, established Sabbath rest, forbade intermarriage with pagan foreigners, and so recovered the special identity of Israel as God's chosen people.

Nehemiah could organize projects and people. Before setting plans he did a careful survey of resources and personnel. Some would have called it unglamorous paper pushing, time-consuming research studies, but Nehemiah called it careful preparation. He then established key objectives, assigned those to responsible leaders (men of faith and piety), and set them to work. All of this opened the leadership potential of others.

Nehemiah faced up to opposition without forcing a violent confrontation. He took insults, innuendo, intimidation, and treachery. He walked through it with his head high and his eyes wide open, with much prayer (Nehemiah 4:9). When he could, he simply ignored the adversary. Always he took precaution. Never did he allow opposition to deflect his energy from the central task. Always he kept faith in God (Nehemiah 4:20).

The test of spiritual leadership is the achievement of its objective. In Nehemiah's case, the record is clear:

"So the wall was completed" (Nehemiah 6:15).

FOR REFLECTION

A. How would you describe at least two major areas in your life that challenge you to accept and exercise leadership?

B. What quality in Nehemiah do you admire the most? Why?

C. What achieved objectives (completed walls) do you desire to leave behind by the time your life is done?

A FINAL WORD

Do you remember the questions and desires that motivated you to open this book? Were they questions about the wisdom of taking up leadership responsibilities or questions about setting them aside? Were you looking at a "breach in the wall" or considering an invitation to lead and wondering if you should step up? Were you wondering if you have what it takes to lead or wondering if you still have what it takes to lead?

Now you know that even though there's a lot involved in leadership, there's even more involved in spiritual leadership. If you feel overwhelmed as you finish this book, welcome to the life of a follower of Jesus. If spiritual leadership were easy, everyone would be doing it!

Spiritual leadership is not a calling we choose to pursue; it is a calling we choose to answer. We don't decide to become leaders; we decide to respond and keep responding to God's call in our lives. Along the way, whether we like it or not, that involves us in leadership.

The account of Nehemiah that closed this book presents the high bar of spiritual leadership—the kind of thoughtful, heartfelt, and wise practices we strive to emulate. But of all the biblical leaders whose style we've examined in these pages, the disciple Peter perhaps best represents many of the struggles we face on a day-to-day basis. One of the benefits we get from knowing Peter's life comes when we listen in on the last, crucial supervisory session between Peter and Jesus. Jesus helped Peter to clarify his commitment: "Simon son of John, do you truly love me more than these?" (John 21:15). Jesus restated Peter's job description: "Feed my lambs" (John 21:15). And Jesus gave Peter a central, overriding, "default" command: "Follow me!" (John 21:19).

Through all the highs and lows of leadership, in times of great certainty and crippling uncertainty, those who have led in rebuilding broken-down walls and bringing God's message of light and life into dark places have been those whose souls have never ceased to say "Yes" to Jesus' invitation, "Follow me." And many of them turned out to be spiritual leaders. What answer to Jesus' invitation echoes in your heart and life today?

CHAPTER NOTES

Chapter 1
1. Stephen Neill, "Address to Ordinands," *The Record*, 28 March 1947, 161. Neill (1900–1984) served in South India and later taught missiology.
2. C. W. Hall, *Samuel Logan Brengle* (New York: Salvation Army, 1933), 274. Brengle (1860–1939) was internationally sought as a holiness speaker during the early decades of this century.

Chapter 2
1. Henry George Liddell (1811–1898) was dean of Christ Church, Oxford University, and chaplain to the Queen. Lewis Carroll wrote *Alice in Wonderland* for Liddell's daughter Alice.
2. Quoted in Paul E. Sangster, *Doctor Sangster* (London: Epworth, 1962), 109. William Sangster (1900–1960) was a leader in British Methodism.
3. Samuel Logan Brengle, *The Soul-Winner's Secret* (London: Salvation Army, 1918), 22.

Chapter 3
1. Paul S. Rees, "The Community Clue," *Life of Faith*, 26 September 1976, 3.

Chapter 4
1. Bernard L. Montgomery, *Memoirs of Field-Marshal Montgomery* (Cleveland: World, 1958), 70. Bernard Law Montgomery (1887–1976) made his mark in World War II as the first allied general to inflict a decisive defeat on the Axis at El Alamein in Northern Africa, October 1942. He was knighted that November.

   Chester Nimitz (1885–1966), quoted in Sanders's text without a citation, was commander of the Pacific Fleet and Pacific Ocean Areas during World War II.

   Charles George Gordon (1833–1885), also quoted without citation, was an eccentric but effective British military commander in China during the 1860s (for which he was tagged "Chinese Gordon") and in Africa, where he died at Khartoum trying to withstand an overwhelming army led by the Mahdi, a mystic leader in the Sudan.
2. Lettie B. Cowman, *Charles E. Cowman* (Los Angeles: Oriental Missionary Society, 1928), 251. John R. Mott (1865–1955) was a Methodist evangelist who served in the Student Volunteer Movement and the YMCA. His best-known book is *Evangelizing the World in Our Generation* (1900), which was also the motto he was widely known for. He was a founder of the World Council of Churches.
3. P. T. Chandapilla was general secretary for the Union of Evangelical Students of India from 1956–1971. His goal was to reach India's intellectuals with the gospel. Following Hudson Taylor, Chandapilla never asked for financial help. He worked closely with InterVarsity Fellowship and the International Fellowship of Evangelical Students.
4. Montgomery, *Memoirs*, 70.

5. Phyllis Thompson, *D. E. Hoste* (London: China Inland Mission, n.d.), 122.
6. A. W. Tozer, in *The Reaper*, February 1962, 459. Aiden Wilson Tozer (1897–1963) was a minister in the Christian and Missionary Alliance. Among his thirty books, the best known is *The Pursuit of God* (1948).
7. Paul E. Sangster, *Doctor Sangster* (London: Epworth, 1962), 109.
8. James Burns, *Revivals, Their Laws and Leaders* (London: Hodder & Stoughton, 1909), 95.
9. Montgomery, *Memoirs*, 70.
10. B. Matthews, *John R. Mott* (London: S.C.M. Press, 1934), 346.
11. John Geddie (1815–1872), born in Scotland, was called the father of foreign missions in the Presbyterian church in Canada. He went as a missionary to the New Hebrides (formerly called Aneityum) in 1848.
12. Matthews, *Mott*, 353.

Chapter 5

1. R. E. Thompson, in *World Vision*, December 1966, 4.

Chapter 6

1. William Barclay, *Letters to Timothy and Titus* (Edinburgh: St. Andrews, 1960), 92. Jeremy Taylor (1613–1667) was an Anglican bishop and chaplain to Charles I. He is known today for his devotional writings, especially *Holy Living* (1650) and *Holy Dying* (1651) written after Charles was beheaded and the victorious Oliver Cromwell was at his peak. Taylor was one of the most popular preachers of his day.

    Mencius (ca.372–289 B.C.), the Chinese philosopher mentioned without citation in the third paragraph, was Confucius's greatest disciple. He promoted the cardinal virtues of love, righteousness, decorum, and wisdom. His Latinized name comes from Meng-Tzu, meaning Master Meng. He was known as the Second Sage.
2. C. W. Hall, *Samuel Logan Brengle* (New York: Salvation Army, 1933), 112.
3. John William Fletcher (1729–1785) was vicar of Madeley in Shropshire. Swiss by birth, he joined the Methodist movement within the Church of England. He is remembered for his sanctity and his devotion to work among coal miners.
4. William Hendriksen, *1 and 2 Timothy and Titus* (London: Banner of Truth, 1959), 36.

    Dietrich Bonhoeffer, quoted but not cited, was a leader in Germany's underground church during the Third Reich. He was executed by the Nazis in 1945 just before Allied troops reached his prison camp.
5. Quoted in Barclay, *Letters*, 86.

Chapter 7

1. William Barclay, *The Letters of Peter and Jude* (Edinburgh: St. Andrews, 1958), 156.
2. Paul S. Rees, *Triumphant in Trouble* (London: Marshall, Morgan & Scott, n.d.), 126.
3. J. H. Jowett, *The Epistles of Peter* (London: Hodder & Stoughton, n.d.), 188. Jowett (1863–1923), an English Congregationalist minister, was pastor of Fifth Avenue Presbyterian Church in New York, then succeeded G. Campbell Morgan at Westminster Chapel in London.

4. Stephen Neill, *On the Ministry* (n.p., n.d.), 107–8. Bishop of Azariah (1874–1945) was the first Indian bishop in the Anglican church. He founded the Missionary Society of Tinnevelly in 1903, then cofounded the National Missionary Society for the evangelization of India.

Chapter 8

1. James Burns, *Revivals, Their Laws and Leaders* (London: Hodder & Stoughton, 1909), 182. Martin Luther (1483–1546) is generally credited with beginning the Protestant Reformation when he nailed "95 Theses" (statements outlining his understanding of the Scriptures contrasted to church teachings) on the church door at Wittenberg, Germany, in October 1517. Adoniram Judson (1788–1850), mentioned earlier, is widely known as a pioneer missionary to Burma.

2. Gustav Warneck (1834–1910) is generally recognized as the founder of the field of study called missiology. He held Germany's first university chair of mission, at Halle, in 1896.

3. Donald Grey Barnhouse (1895–1960) worked in Belgium and France before taking the pastorate of Tenth Presbyterian Church in Philadelphia. He edited *Revelation*, later *Eternity* magazine, and wrote extensively.

4. Amy Wilson Carmichael (1867–1951), missionary to India, founded the Dohnavur Fellowship to help neglected and abused children. Born in Ireland, she became the first woman to be supported on the mission field by the Keswick Missions Committee. She served fifty-six years without a furlough and wrote thirty-five books.

5. Phyllis Thompson, *Climbing on Track* (London: China Inland Mission, 1954), 116.

6. Florence Nightingale (1820–1910) was the heroine of the Crimean War and founder of modern nursing. Born to Italian nobility, she felt called to serve God at age seventeen and abandoned her family's wealth and privilege. Adulation flowed from her work in Scutari, Turkey, on behalf of British troops. She became a recluse, however, for the last four decades of her life.

7. N. G. Dunning, *Samuel Chadwick* (London: Hodder & Stoughton, 1934), 15. Chadwick lived from 1860 to 1932.

8. J. R. Andrews, *George Whitefield* (London: Morgan & Scott, 1915), 410–11. Barclay Buxton (1860–1946) mentioned immediately after this citation, was a missionary to Japan for forty-six years.

9. *World Vision*, January 1966, 5.

10. Brooke Foss Westcott (1825–1901) worked for twenty-eight years with Fenton Hort on *The New Testament in the Original Greek* (1881). His Bible commentaries are still read.

11. Powhatten James, *George W. Truett* (Nashville: Broadman, 1953), 266. Truett lived from 1867 to 1944.

12. Lettie B. Cowman, *Charles E. Cowman* (Los Angeles: Oriental Missionary Society, 1928), 259. Charles Cowman founded the Oriental Missionary Society, now known as OMS International, in 1901. Lettie Cowman wrote *Streams in the Desert*, one of the most-read devotional books of all time. William McKinley (1843–1901), mentioned immediately after this citation, was the twenty-fifth president of the United States. He died from an assassin's bullet wound suffered in Buffalo, New York.

13. W. H. T. Gairdner, *Douglas M. Thornton* (London: Hodder & Stoughton, n.d.), 80. Thornton (1873–1907) was educational secretary for the Student Volunteer Missionary Union.

  Henry Martyn (1781–1812), mentioned in the previous paragraph, was inspired to a life in missions after reading the diary of David Brainerd. He served as chaplain to the East India Company in Bengal, and translated the New Testament into Hindustani.

  Albert Benjamin Simpson (1844–1915) founded the Evangelical Missionary Alliance, later the Christian and Missionary Alliance, and wrote over seventy books.
14. Marcus Lane, *Archbishop Mowll* (London: Hodder & Stoughton, 1960), 202. Howard West Kilvington Mowll (1890–1958) served as an Anglican bishop in Canada, China, and Sydney (Australia).
15. Dunning, *Chadwick*, 20.
16. Theodore Roosevelt, in B. Matthews, *John R. Mott* (London: S.C.M. Press, 1934), 355. Roosevelt (1858–1919) was twenty-sixth president of the United States.
17. Phyllis Thompson, *D. E. Hoste* (London: China Inland Mission, n.d.), 155.
18. David Livingstone (1813–1873) began work in a cotton mill at age twelve, but taught himself Greek, theology, and medicine. In 1840 he went to Africa under the London Missionary Society. He was found by journalist Henry Stanley, working for the New York Herald, in 1871. Stanley greeted the missionary with the simple yet oft-quoted words: "Doctor Livingstone, I presume."
19. Burns, *Revivals*, 181–82.
20. Ibid., 167–68. Luther's precise words at the Diet of Worms are the subject of historians' debates. Sanders' original text quotes from Burns. More recent historical data was used for the quotation in this edition. See James M. Kittelson, "The Accidental Revolutionary," in *Christian History*, Issue 34, 16. Quotations preceding Worms and near the time of Luther's death are reported as they appear in Burns.
21. William Law (1686–1761) was an evangelical devotional writer and mystic. He is best known for *A Serious Call to a Devout and Holy Life* (1728).
22. C. W. Hall, *Samuel Logan Brengle* (New York: Salvation Army, 1933), 275.
23. Robert Morrison (1782–1834) was an interpreter for the East India Company in Canton. He translated the Bible into Cantonese, and labored for twenty-seven years in China for about a dozen converts.

Chapter 9

1. Quoted in C. W. Hall, *Samuel Logan Brengle* (New York: Salvation Army, 1933), 278. Samuel Johnson (1709–1784), mentioned earlier, was an English poet, essayist, and lexicographer. His *Dictionary of the English Language* (1747) was the standard for a century.
2. Helmut Thielecke, *Encounter with Spurgeon* (Philadelphia: Fortress, 1963), 26. Charles Haddon Spurgeon (1834–1892), one of the best-known preachers of the nineteenth century, was pastor of the Metropolitan Tabernacle in London for thirty-two years.
3. A. E. Norrish, *Christian Leadership* (New Delhi: Masihi Sabiyata Sanstha, 1963), 28.
4. *Latin America Evangelist*, May–June 1965.
5. Robert E. Speer, *Christ and Life* (New York: Revell, 1901), 103. Frederick William Robertson (1816–1853) was ordained in the Church of England in 1840 and made his

mark as a preacher among the working poor of Brighton. William Wilberforce (1759–1833), mentioned earlier, was a member of the British parliament whose work, strongly opposed by vested interest, eventually led to laws prohibiting slavery and the slave trade. In 1804 he helped form the British and Foreign Bible Society.

6. Ibid., 104. Joseph Butler (1692–1752), Anglican bishop, is remembered for his book *Analogy of Religion* (1736), probably the best defense of Christian faith to appear in the eighteenth century.

7. William Barclay, *Letters of Peter and Jude* (Edinburgh: St. Andrews, 1960), 258. John Chrysostom (ca.347–407), mentioned earlier, is an "early church father." He was for ten years a monastic hermit, then deacon and priest in Antioch, then patriarch of Constantinople. He was exiled for preaching against vice and excess among the clergy and royalty.

8. J. C. Pollock, *Hudson Taylor and Maria* (London: Hodder & Stoughton, 1962), 35.

9. Ernest Gordon, *A. J. Gordon* (London: Hodder & Stoughton, 1897), 191.

10. Phyllis Thompson, *D. E. Hoste* (London: China Inland Mission, n.d.), 158.

11. A. E. Thompson, *The Life of A. B. Simpson* (Harrisburg, PA: Christian Publications, 1920), 204.

12. H. C. Lees, *St. Paul's Friends* (London: Religious Tract Society, 1917), 11.

13. A. W. Tozer, *Let My People Go* (Harrisburg, PA: Christian Publications, 1957), 36.

14. S. P. Carey, *William Carey* (London: Hodder & Stoughton), 1923), 256.

15. Lettie B. Cowman, *Charles E. Cowman* (Los Angeles: Oriental Missionary Society, 1928), 269.

16. Mrs. Hudson Taylor, *Pastor Hsi* (London: China Inland Mission, 1949), 164, 167.

17. Mark Clark (1896–1984) was a lieutenant general in the U.S. Army during World War II. He commanded the Fifth Army during the Italian campaign, and was commander of all United Nations troops in Korea during that conflict.

18. George Adam Smith, *The Book of Isaiah* (London: Hodder & Stoughton, n.d.), 229.

19. James Burns, *Revival, Their Laws and Leaders* (London: Hodder & Stoughton, 1909), 311.

20. *World Vision*, February 1966, 5.

Chapter 10

1. A. T. Pierson, *The Acts of the Holy Spirit* (London: Morgan & Scott, n.d.), 63. Arthur Tappan Pierson (1837–1911) was a preacher, writer, and missionary spokesman who also served as a consultant on the Scofield Reference Bible.

2. D. J. Fant, *A. W. Tozer* (Harrisburg, PA: Christian Publications, 1964), 73, 83.

Chapter 11

1. N.G. Dunning, *Samuel Chadwick* (London: Hodder & Stoughton, 1934), 19.

2. D.M. McIntyre, *The Prayer Life of Our Lord* (London: Morgan & Scott, n.d.), 30–31.

3. George Mueller (1805–1898) was a Plymouth Brethren leader who refused a salary, believing that God would supply his needs by prayer alone. He established an orphanage in Bristol for two thousand youngsters on the strength of prayer and promoted prayer during a seventeen-year world tour.

4. E. M. Bounds, *Prayer and Praying Men* (London: Hodder & Stoughton, 1921). Edward McKendree Bounds (1835–1913) was an American Methodist Episcopal minister who served churches throughout the South. He was a captain in the Confederate army.

Chapter 12

1. Michelangelo (1475–1564) was an Italian sculptor, painter, and poet. His famous works include the statue "David" and the ceiling of the Sistine Chapel in the Vatican. William James (1842–1910) was a Harvard psychologist and philosopher generally credited with popularizing a new approach to knowledge called pragmatism.
2. Mary Slessor (1848–1915) went to Calabar, West Africa, in 1876, a region not controlled by any colonial power. Her sense of humor and courage won the confidence of warring chiefs, and she contributed immensely to the life of children and women.
3. J. Stuart Holden, *The Gospel of the Second Chance* (London: Marshall Brothers, 1912), 188.
4. W. Y. Fullerton, *F. B. Meyer* (London: Marshall, Morgan & Scott, n.d.), 70. Frederick Brotherton Meyer (1847–1929) was a Baptist preacher with a worldwide pulpit and a base in London. He was known for crusades against prostitution, alcoholic beverages, and prizefighting, and on behalf of unwanted children and unmarried mothers. John Wesley (1703–1791) is well known as the energetic cofounder of Methodism.
5. Paul E. Sangster, *Doctor Sangster* (London: Epworth, 1962), 314.
6. *Sunday School Times*, 22 November 1913, 713.

Chapter 13

1. William Tyndale (ca.1494–1536) was the first to translate the New Testament into English, in 1525, from a base in Germany. He was arrested in 1535 and a year later burned at the stake. Before his death, he completed the translation of the first five Old Testament books and Jonah.
2. A. W. Tozer, "The Use and Abuse of Books," *The Alliance Weekly*, 22 February 1956, 2.
3. Harold J. Ockenga, *Christianity Today*, 4 March 1966, 36.
4. Francis Bacon, quoted in *The Alliance Weekly*, 14 March 1956, 2. Bacon (1561–1626) was a statesman and scholar who served Elizabeth I and James I. His many writings deal with scientific method, political theory, and the history of ideas. He was a loyal member of the Church of England.
5. Charles Finney (1792–1875) was trained in law but turned to ministry after his conversion in 1821. He led revivals through the Northeast, pastored churches, wrote books, opposed slavery and drink, and was president of Oberlin College from 1851–1866. The book cited here was published in 1835.
6. C. W. Hall, *Samuel Logan Brengle* (New York: Salvation Army, 1933), 269.
7. Charles Thomas Studd (1862–1931) inherited a fortune, but gave it away and sailed to China as a missionary in 1885. He also served in India and Africa, and helped found the Student Volunteer Movement.
8. Muriel Ormrod, *The Reaper*, August 1965, 229.
9. Helmut Thielecke, *Encounter with Spurgeon* (Philadelphia: Fortress, 1963), 197.
10. *Sunday School Times*, 22 November 1913, 715.

Chapter 14

1. The reference is to John Bunyan's *Pilgrim's Progress*, published in 1678 and now translated into hundreds of languages. Bunyan (1628–1688) wrote more than sixty books.

Chapter 15

1. Robert E. Speer, *Marks of a Man* (New York: Revell, 1907), 109.
2. Samuel Logan Brengle, *The Soul-Winner's Secret* (London: Salvation Army, 1918), 23.
3. The reference is to the famous 1925 book, *The Man Nobody Knows*, written by advertising advocate Bruce Barton. The book purported to show that Jesus was the keenest business mind, and hence the most successful salesman, of all time. Jesus' techniques could revolutionize the world, Barton argued.
4. Samuel M. Zwemer, *It Is Hard to Be a Christian* (London: Marshalls, 1937), 139. Samuel Marinus Zwemer (1867–1952) established missions to Muslims in the Middle East and was later professor of the history of religion at Princeton Seminary. He wrote over fifty books.
5. Lettie Cowman, *Charles E. Cowman* (Los Angeles: Oriental Missionary Society, 1928), 260.
6. Used by permission of the Christian Literature Crusade, Fort Washington, Pennsylvania.
7. Friedrich Nietzsche (1844–1900) was raised Lutheran, but as a scholar and university professor of philosophy, he became one of the most well-known atheists of the modern era. In every way he found reason to criticize Christian faith and life, except that he admired Jesus. Nietzsche went insane in 1889 but continued to publish attacks on the church, its mission, and its ethic.
8. W. H. T. Gairdner, *Douglas M. Thornton* (London: Hodder & Stoughton, n.d.), 225.
9. R. D. Abella, in *Evangelical Thought* (Manila n.d.).
10. Phyllis Thompson, *Climbing on Track* (London: China Inland Mission, 1954), 116.
11. C. W. Hall, *Samuel Logan Brengle* (New York: Salvation Army, 1933), 272.
12. J. Gregory Mantle, *Beyond Humiliation* (Chicago: Moody, n.d.), 140–141.
13. Cowman, *Cowman*, 258.
14. Phyllis Thompson, *D. E. Hoste* (London: China Inland Mission, n.d.), 130–31.
15. Thompson, *Climbing on Track*, 115.

Chapter 16

1. Alexander Balmain Bruce (1831–1899) was professor of apologetics and New Testament at the Free Church College, Glasgow, from 1868 to 1899. He wrote *Training of the Twelve* in 1871.
2. Phyllis Thompson, *D. E. Hoste* (London: China Inland Mission, n.d.), 217.
3. Ibid., 158.
4. In *The Reaper*, May 1961, 89. Robert Louis Stevenson (1850–1894) was a British writer best known for *Treasure Island* and *Dr. Jekyll and Mr. Hyde*.
5. Marcus Loane, *Archbishop Mowll* (London: Hodder & Stoughton, 1960), 249.
6. Edward White Benson (1829–1896) became archbishop of Canterbury in 1882. His leadership of the Church of England was marked by concerns for education and the church in Wales.

Chapter 17

1. Used by permission of Evangelical Publishers, Toronto, Canada.
2. Alexander Maclaren (1826–1910) was pastor for forty-five years at Union Chapel in Manchester, England. He was the first president of the Baptist World Alliance in 1905.
3. James Anthony Froude (1818–1894) was a British writer and historian attached to the Oxford Movement.

Chapter 18

1. Dwight L. Moody (1837–1899) was one of America's foremost evangelists. He rose to national prominence after success in preaching meetings in Scotland and England during 1873–1875. He established educational institutions in Northfield, Massachusetts, and Chicago, Illinois (later called Moody Bible Institute).
2. Phyllis Thompson, *D. E. Hoste* (London: China Inland Mission, n.d.). 56.
3. A. E. Thompson, *The Life of A. B. Simpson* (Harrisburg, PA: Christian Publications, 1920), 208.
4. B. Matthews, *John R. Mott* (London: Hodder & Stoughton, 1909), 364.
5. Paul E. Sangster, *Doctor Sangster* (London: Epworth, 1962), 88, 221.
6. Phyllis Thompson, *Climbing on Track* (London: China Inland Mission, 1954), 99.

Chapter 19

1. *Sunday School Times*, 8 November 1913, 682. Lyman Beecher (1775–1863) was one of America's leading revival preachers, a New England pastor, and president of Lane Seminary.
2. A. E. Thompson, *The Life of A. B. Simpson* (Harrisburg, PA: Christian Publications, 1920), 208.

Chapter 20

1. Lesslie Newbigin, in *International Review of Missions*, April 1950. Newbigin retired after forty years of missionary service in India.
2. H. C. Lees, *St. Paul's Friends* (London: Religious Tract Society, 1917), 135–41.
3. Paul S. Rees, "The Community Clue," *Life of Faith*, 26 September 1976, 3.
4. P. Howard, *Frank Buchman* (London: Heineman, 1961), 111. Frank Nathan Daniel Buchman (1878–1961) was a Lutheran minister who, discouraged with his work, moved to England in 1908. There he came in contact with the Keswick movement and experienced a conversion. In 1938 he launched the Moral Rearmament movement to promote love, honesty, purity, and unselfishness. The movement endured criticism from conservative Christians for alleged humanism. In Sanders's first edition, he makes a point of not endorsing "the merits" of Buchman's movement.
5. W. H. T. Gairdner, *Douglas M. Thornton* (London: Hodder & Stoughton, n.d.), 121.

Chapter 21

1. Robert Louis Stevenson, in *The Reaper*, July 1942, 96.
2. Stephen Neill, in *The Record*, 28 March 1947, 161.

3. Helmut Thielecke, *Encounter with Spurgeon* (Philadelphia: Fortress, 1963).

4. W. Y. Fullerton, *F. B. Meyer* (London: Marshall, Morgan & Scott, n.d.), 172.

5. Quoted in Thielecke, *Encounter*, 219.

6. N. G. Dunning, *Samuel Chadwick* (London: Hodder & Stoughton, 1934), 206.

7. H. C. A. Dixon, *A. C. Dixon* (New York: Putnam's, 1931), 277. Amzi Clarence Dixon (1854–1925) served as pastor of Moody Memorial Church and the Metropolitan Tabernacle of London.

8. Ibid., 158. Reuben Archer Torrey (1856–1928), a Congregationalist minister, was first superintendent of the Moody Bible Institute (then called Chicago Evangelistic Society) and pastor of Moody Memorial Church (then Chicago Avenue Church). He conducted crusades in Europe, Asia, and the Orient. He was later president of the Bible Institute of Los Angeles (now Biola College) and pastor of Church of the Open Door in downtown Los Angeles.

9. Charles Hodge (1797–1878), quoted here without citation, was professor of theology at Princeton Seminary. A conservative Presbyterian on matters of doctrine, he also believed that the Bible permitted slavery and condemned only its abuse, a position that caused him immense controversy during the peak of his career.

A SMALL GROUP
STUDY GUIDE FOR

SPIRITUAL LEADERSHIP

*S*piritual Leadership has proven to be a helpful book for almost everyone who wants to identify and improve his or her leadership abilities. But study and discussion of the book with a small group of close friends can bring even greater benefit. It will encourage honesty and increase accountability. While Sanders makes the case that godly leadership is a God-given assignment, God's Word indicates that He often uses the confirmation of others along the way (see Acts 13:1–3). This study guide was developed to allow small groups to discuss the concepts in the book in six sessions. The questions are intended to expand upon the reflection questions found at the end of each chapter. The format for each session is divided into three parts.

Get Started starts with common life experiences and helps all group members get involved in the discussion. For a one hour session, spend no more than five minutes on these questions.

Get the Point focuses on the main point of three or four chapters in the book, and provides further discussion on key Bible passages. These questions will typically require 40–45 minutes of discussion time.

Get Going moves group members into the action phase with suggestions for life application. Reserve about 10–15 minutes to discuss these questions.

Have each group member read the chapters and prepare their answers prior to the small group meeting. Encourage listening by asking the group members to respond to what others are sharing. The sessions are intended for more than each participant giving their answers to the questions. Be sure to open and close your discussion time with prayer.

STUDY ONE

Read chapters 1–3 in *Spiritual Leadership*, then prepare answers to the following questions for group discussion.

Get Started

1. Tell about a time you aspired to be a leader in some area of life. What position did you aspire to? What happened?

Get the Point

2. Why is it difficult for Christians today to wholeheartedly agree with Paul that spiritual leadership is "an honorable ambition"? (chapter 1)

3. Why are spiritual leaders of the kind we see in Scripture in such short supply today? (chapter 2)

4. What is the role of leadership training if spiritual leadership is conferred by God alone? (chapter 2)

5. How do the leadership qualities admired in the business world compare to the qualities required for spiritual leaders? Read and include insights from Mark 10:41–45 in discussing this question.

6. How would you describe "servant leadership" to a young, successful entrepreneur who recently became a Christian? (chapter 3)

7. How would your church be different if it identified, encouraged, and expected the spiritual leadership described in this chapter? (chapter 3)

8. What is the most significant insight about spiritual leadership that you have gained by reading these first three chapters?

Get Going
9. What personal ambitions for leadership do you need to restrain? Which need reinforcement?

10. Where do you most need to exhibit an attitude of selfless service?

STUDY TWO

Read chapters 4–7 in *Spiritual Leadership*, then prepare answers to the following questions for group discussion.

Get Started

1. What "natural" leadership qualities have others pointed out in you? What have you done with those observations?

Get the Point

2. In your opinion, what is a key difference between natural leadership and spiritual leadership? (chapter 4)

3. How is natural leadership transformed into spiritual leadership? (chapter 4)

4. Which of the items in Sanders's list on pages 34–36 concern you the most in your own development as a leader? (chapter 5)

5. How does your church decide when someone is fit for spiritual leadership? How well is the process working? (chapter 6)

6. What advice from Paul about leadership did you find most timely at this point in your spiritual development? (chapter 6)

7. What deficiencies and failings do you most often notice in leaders? (chapter 7)

8. Is it important for someone to fail as badly as Peter did, in order to develop a humble heart? How have people you know learned humility? (chapter 7)

9. Who do you prefer as a model of leadership, Peter or Paul? In what ways?

Get Going
10. What one quality of spiritual leadership needs the most attention in your life? How can you get started on it this week?

STUDY THREE

Read chapters 8–10 in *Spiritual Leadership,* then prepare answers to the following questions for group discussion.

Get Started

1. If you were granted a wish and could instantly and permanently acquire one leadership quality, which would you select?

Get the Point

2. How can vision create problems? (chapter 8)

3. Can serious people learn to be funny? Why is it difficult to maintain a sense of humor when leading? (chapter 9)

4. How can anger help a leader? How can it hurt? What did you find helpful about the anger guidelines listed by Bishop Butler on page 68 (chapter 9)

5. Why is patience a particularly difficult virtue for leaders to develop? (chapter 9)

6. What leadership qualities of those described in these chapters do you think are in most short supply among Christians?

7. When faced with a decision to do something or go somewhere, how can a leader tell the difference between promptings from the Holy Spirit and inclinations of the self? (chapter 10)

8. What is the difference between being naturally gifted in leadership and being spiritually gifted? (chapter 10)

Get Going

9. Now that you have reached the midway point in the book, give yourself a report card on your leadership qualities. Where have you made improvement recently? Where do you still need some more work? What spiritual leadership qualities have been confirmed and affirmed in your life?

STUDY FOUR

Read chapters 11–14 in *Spiritual Leadership,* then prepare answers to the following questions for group discussion.

Get Started

1. During an average week, to which of these activities do you give the most time: lawn care/house projects? book/magazine/newspaper reading? television/movie viewing? prayer?

Get the Point

2. When have you felt sorrowful about your prayer life? What changes did you make? (chapter 11)

3. What are some of the obstacles that keep people from prayer? (chapter 11)

4. If time were not a consideration, what work in the church would you most enjoy? (chapter 12)

5. Why do spiritual leaders often feel undue pressure in the use of time? (chapter 12)

6. If you were stranded on an island, what three books (or magazines) would you most desire? (chapter 13)

7. If the notes and files of your reading were to be turned over to a detective-psychologist for character analysis, what would they conclude about you? (chapter 13)

8. What does it mean to lead with intensity? How does this relate to the word "zeal" as the Bible uses it? How does a person learn to do this? (chapter 14)

9. Discuss the idea that spiritual leadership is always from the front, never from the rear or sidelines. How does servant-leadership fit here? What extremes pose dangers for this view? What problems does this view solve? (chapter 14)

Get Going
10. What step could you take this week to start making better use of your time for God's kingdom?

11. Where are you presently investing time that could be better invested in developing your prayer life?

STUDY FIVE

Read chapters 15–18 in *Spiritual Leadership,* then prepare answers to the following questions for group discussion.

Get Started

1. Leadership can be difficult and demanding. Is this always true? If so, what price are you willing to pay?

Get the Point

2. What does it mean for a leader to take up his or her cross? (chapter 15)

3. How should leaders handle just criticism and rejection? (chapter 15)

4. How many of Benson's rules for living are you already practicing? Which are the most difficult for you to follow? (chapter 16)

5. What's the difference between good compromise (the opposite of stubbornness) and bad compromise (the opposite of commitment)? How can you tell when compromise is right and good? (chapter 17)

6. How long does it take you to overcome the feeling of failure? With whom do you discuss failure? (chapter 17)

7. Which test of leadership (compromise, ambition, impossible situations, failure, jealousy) do you fear the most? Why? (chapter 17)

8. How do you know that you have communicated instructions carefully enough? How can your ambiguities in delegation return to haunt you? (chapter 18)

9. What do you do, or where do you go, for renewal from fatigue?

Get Going
10. What steps can you take this week to better prepare you for the tests of leadership you may eventually face in the future?

STUDY SIX

Read chapters 19–22 in *Spiritual Leadership*, then prepare answers to the following questions for group discussion.

Get Started

1. What changes have been difficult for you in the past year? At work? At church? At home? In what ways have these difficulties been related to leadership?

Get the Point

2. As you look back, how have you seen God at work preparing you for leadership? How has He used you to prepare others for leadership? (chapter 19)

3. From what have you "retired" because your best contribution was over or the time was ripe for another leader? What were your feelings? (chapter 19)

4. What dangers do popularity hold for a leader? (chapter 20)

5. Which of the perils of leadership worry you the most? (chapter 21)

6. What areas of "moderation" have you identified as crucial to your fitness for spiritual service? (chapter 21)

7. How do you deal with people who believe they are never wrong? (chapter 21)

8. What do you most admire about Nehemiah's leadership? (chapter 22)

9. When you look ahead to the end of your life, what "walls" do you want to see standing? (chapter 22)

10. To what degree should men and women aspire to different leadership roles?

Get Going
11. How can you direct your own energies to better do the work God has *for you*?

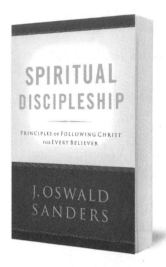

"Come, follow me," Jesus said, "and I will make you fishers of men."

Jesus' first call to those who would become His followers was a call to discipleship. Most Christians desire a life that brings glory and honor to God, yet few fully understand the sacrifice Christ asks of a true disciple.

Containing study questions at the end of the text, this book provides probing insight into the biblical requirements for a disciple in the Lord's service.

ISBN-10: 0-8024-6798-9
ISBN-13: 978-0-8024-6798-0

The biblical mandate for believers is clear— to grow from spiritual infancy to maturity.

"The New Testament knows three types of Christians," notes J. Oswald Sanders.

"The spiritually mature, the spiritually immature, and the spiritually decadent. It is tragically possible for the believer either to fall short of maturity or to fall back from it."

Complete with scriptural principles for spiritual development and study questions at the end of the text, this classic handbook is a timeless treasure.

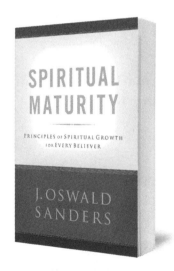

ISBN-10: 0-8024-6794-6
ISBN-13: 978-0-8024-6794-2

Find these other books by J. Oswald Sanders
at your favorite local or online bookstore.
www.MoodyPublishers.com

INDEX OF PERSONS

Index of Scripture